ISBN 978-1-330-26757-8
PIBN 10007236

FB &c Ltd, Dalton House, 60 Windsor Avenue, London, SW19 2RR.
Company number 08720141. Registered in England and Wales.

For support please visit www.forgottenbooks.com

EXPLANATION OF THE FRONTISPIECE.

VIEW OF THE AIR-PASSAGES IN THE ACT OF SINGING. THE POSITION OF THE UVULA IS THAT TAKEN IN THE DELIVERY OF THE HIGHER CHEST NOTES. IN HEAD TONES IT IS DRAWN STILL FURTHER UPWARDS.

(Diagram modified from Bellamy's edition of *Braune's Anatomical Plates.*)

a, frontal sinus; *b*, sphenoidal sinus; *c*, lower, middle, and upper nasal meatus; *d*, opening of the Eustachian tube; *f*, uvula; *e*, pharynx; *g*, tongue; *h*, epiglottis; *i*, vocal cord; j, j^1, j^2, windpipe; *k*, lung; *l*, liver, with the cut edge of the diaphragm just above it, separating it from the base of *k*, the lung. The canal behind j, j^1, j^2, is the gullet, or food-passage, leading down to the stomach.

OPINIONS OF THE PRESS ON PREVIOUS EDITIONS.

"It is compiled by a scientific man of the first order, whose facts and deductions may be accepted without a moment's hesitation. Dr. Mackenzie, as is well known, is the guide, philosopher, and friend of almost the entire musical profession. . . . Golden rules might be multiplied *ad infinitum* from Dr. Mackenzie's pages, but sufficient has been said to show that his work is as useful and readable as it is scientifically important."—*Times.*

"Thought, learning, long experience, quick and constant observation, and a play of mind which keeps it free from all mere trammels of theory—such are the qualifications which the author of this little manual brought to the task of writing it."—*St. James's Gazette.*

"The book may be recommended as a wholesome antidote to those new treatises which are now constantly appearing with respect to the training and care of the singing voice, and which, while loaded with much scientific jargon, are hopelessly bewildering to the real voice trainer."—*Saturday Review.*

"As a guide to health management, it is invaluable for singers and speakers."—*Church Times.*

"We can confidently recommend the book to all singing students." *The Musical World.*

"A chapter headed 'Special Hygiene for Singers' contains valuable hints on temperance, clothing, diet, exercise and many other matters absolutely necessary to be carefully studied by vocalists."—*The Musical Times.*

"Valuable hints for training the voice are given."—*Nature.*

"The book contains many practical hints, both for singers and speakers, and the whole work, as might be expected, shows evidence of large experience and extensive reading."—*British Medical Journal.*

"It combines in a happy manner all the excellences of a thoroughly correct and scientific work, with the best style of popular writing and lucid exposition. No speaker or vocalist should neglect to add it to his or her book-shelf."—*Health.*

THE HYGIENE

OF

THE VOCAL ORGANS.

A Practical Handbook

FOR

SINGERS AND SPEAKERS.

BY

MORELL MACKENZIE, M.D. LOND.,

Consulting Physician to the Hospital for Diseases of the Throat;
Formerly Physician and Lecturer on Physiology, at the London Hospital:
Physician to the Royal Society of Musicians.

FOURTH EDITION

London:
MACMILLAN AND CO.
AND NEW YORK.
1887.

" La voix est un son humain que rien d'inanimé ne saurait parfaitement contrefaire. Elle a une autorité et une propriété d'insinuation qui manquent à l'écriture. Ce n'est pas seulement de l'air, c'est de l'air modulé par nous, imprégné de notre chaleur, et comme enveloppé par la vapeur de notre atmosphère, dont quelque émanation l'accompagne et qui lui donne une certaine configuration et de certaines vertus propres à agir sur l'esprit."—JOUBERT.

" Præterradit enim vox fauceis sæpe facitque
Asperiora foras gradiens arteria clamor.
Quippe per angustum turba majore coorta
Ire foras ubi cœperunt primordia vocum,
Scilicet expletis quoque janua raditur oris
Rauca viis, et iter lædit quâ vox it in auras."

LUCRETIUS, lib. iv. 532-7.

PREFACE TO THE FOURTH EDITION.

THE demand for this little work continues to be so great that another edition is already called for. The alterations are confined to a few corrections in the Index.

April 1887.

PREFACE TO THE THIRD EDITION.

SIX weeks after the publication of the second edition of this volume a third was called for, so that it would not appear that much alteration or addition was required. Nevertheless I have thought it desirable to make a few slight changes, the principal of which consist in placing the anatomy of the vocal organs and the chapter on the conflicting views on the falsetto register each in a separate appendix at the end of the volume. The large demand for this little work has also led me to add an index, which I trust will be found useful.

19, HARLEY STREET,
February, 1887.

PREFACE TO THE SECOND EDITION.

IN issuing a second edition of this handbook the Author cannot refrain from expressing his gratification at the favourable reception which it has met with from those best qualified to judge. It is a source of legitimate pleasure to him to find his humble efforts so favourably acknowledged by the press, and by public and private teachers.

The present edition is substantially a reprint of the first. One or two verbal errors have been corrected, and a few slight additions have been made here and there, but there is no material alteration in the text.

PREFACE TO THE FIRST EDITION.

THERE are already so many books on the voice that some wonder may not unreasonably be felt that I should have seen fit to add to the number. By way of explanation I may be allowed to direct the reader's attention to the exact nature and scope of my little work. I have no pretension to speak with authority as a musician or even as a physiologist, and in the following pages I do not profess either to teach singing or elocution, or to throw new light on the obscurer problems of voice-production. Matters belonging to either of these provinces are dealt with only in their relation to the well-being and functional efficiency of the vocal organs. That is a subject on which I may with less presumption claim a hearing. For a quarter of a century I have been engaged in ministering to diseased throats, and every singer or actor of note in this country, with hardly an exception, has at one time or other come under my hands. I have thus had very unusual opportunities of studying the conditions which affect the voice for good or for evil, and my own observation has been assisted and supplemented by the personal experience of vocalists of world-wide celebrity. How I have used my advantages my readers must judge. I wish it, however, to be clearly understood that my point of view is throughout that of the practical physician. I have, therefore, avoided unnecessary technical details, and striven to make the book a really useful guide to those who have to use the voice in the pulpit or in the rostrum, on the stage or in the political arena.

June, 1886.

CONTENTS.

CHAPTER I.

CHAPTER II.

CHAPTER III.

CHAPTER IV.

CHAPTER V.

CHAPTER VI.

CHAPTER VII.

CHAPTER VIII.

APPENDIX I.

APPENDIX II.

APPENDIX III.

LIST OF ILLUSTRATIONS.

THE HYGIENE

OF

THE VOCAL ORGANS.

CHAPTER I.

INTRODUCTORY.

THE art of medicine embraces the two great divisions of hygiene and therapeutics, the former of which deals with the prevention of disease, and the latter with its cure. It is remarkable that whilst in all ages much attention has been given to the treatment of the many ills that flesh is heir to, so little thought has been bestowed on how to ward them off. In spite of innumerable wise saws to the effect that prevention is better than cure, hygiene has until comparatively recent times occupied a merely secondary position. Even the Greeks of old, to whom the body was almost an object of worship, gave Hygieia a subordinate place in the hierarchy of Olympus. Nowadays the supreme importance of hygiene is universally allowed; and the goddess of health-preservation bids fair to take precedence of her father, Æsculapius the healer. In other words, the sanitary engineer is abroad, and threatens to displace the doctor. Half a century ago Carlyle complained that the spirit of the time was mechanical : the present age is nothing if not hygienic. The problems of drainage and ventilation excite a livelier interest than those of "fate, foreknowledge, freedom absolute"; the true evangel is looked for by many in a proper disposal of sewage ; the inventor of an improved trap is more venerated than the discoverer of a new planet. Questions relating to ladies' under-clothing are discussed from the standpoint of advanced physiology, and even the tyrant Fashion is defied by some fair sanitarians who have taken the "divided skirt" as their *oriflamme*. It is not only the health of the body as a whole that is cared for, but the well-being of each and every one of its component parts is zealously studied. Learned professors have not disdained to place the results of painstaking anatomical researches at the service of shoemakers, whilst the skin, the hair, the eye, the teeth, have each been made the text for the conveyance of much good advice by philanthropic men of science. The voice has received its fair share of attention in this outburst of hygienic enthusiasm ; within the last few years doctors and singing-masters seem to have been smitten with an overmastering desire to impart their "own gained knowledge" on the subject to their less privileged fellow men. The result of these well-meant endeavours would be of greater practical value if there were a little more harmony among the teachers. As, however, each succeeding writer appears to make it a point of honour to controvert the statements of his predecessors, the effect on the mind of the anxious student must be as bewildering as the tone in which the discussions are often carried on is distressing to a cultivated intelligence. Some of the publications alluded to no doubt show considerable ability, and embody the results of sound and honest work. Many, however, are neither scientific nor practical, whilst nearly all are too technical to be profitable to the large majority of vocalists.

My aim in this little treatise is to put before the reader, in the simplest way, common-sense rules for the culture and management of the voice, divested of all technical matter beyond what is absolutely required for an intelligent apprehension of the principles on which the rules are founded. A few preliminary remarks on hygiene will help to put the subject in a clearer light. Though the term is usually applied to the prevention of disease, it has in reality a wider meaning. Hygiene has a positive as well as a negative side. The preservation of health means not only that actual mischief is avoided, but that the body is kept in the best working order. Thus the hygiene of sight, for instance, teaches not merely how injury to the eye or impairment of its power may be prevented, but also how the organ may be maintained in a state of functional perfection. Hygiene as applied to the vocal apparatus, therefore, must include a consideration of the best methods of developing its powers to the highest pitch as well as protecting it from injury or decay. *The right use of the voice is the chief factor in the maintenance of its quality.* Many persons suppose that this "comes by nature," as Dogberry thought of reading and writing, but so far from this being the case, it has by the bulk of mankind to be acquired by laborious effort with the help of skilful training. As the health of the voice depends largely on its proper education, this must form the ground-work of every system of vocal hygiene. The subject therefore naturally divides itself into two parts: first, the training and formation of the voice; secondly, the care of the voice when formed. In addition to this the relation of the vocal organs to the general economy must be understood by all who use the voice, and especially by those who undertake to train it. Singers and speakers are not only artists but also in a certain degree athletes, their work consisting essentially in well-ordered muscular movements. A man may be trained for a foot-race or a boxing-match by methods which, while calculated to develop the special qualities required for the performance of the feat, may be simply disastrous to the health of the body as a whole. In like manner an unintelligent teacher may seek to develop the voice at the expense of its owner's constitution. For the avoidance of so dangerous an error—one, moreover, which inevitably defeats its own object—some knowledge of the elementary laws of health is an indispensable part in the equipment of the vocal instructor. It is needless to add that he should be acquainted with the hygienic code more especially applying to the organs which are the instruments of his art.

CHAPTER II.

THE VOICE.

Physiology of the Vocal Organs.

IT would savour of pedantry to give a formal definition of a thing so well known as the voice,[1] but

[1] *Voice* in its broad meaning is *sound produced in the larynx*. It may be well to state that in the following pages I use the word *voice* solely as signifying sound produced by the vibration of the vocal reeds when struck from below by a current of air from the lungs. Various *noises* can no doubt be made by sucking air into the larynx more or less violently from above, and possibly such unnatural phonation could be cultivated to some extent, and would no doubt be admired by many who would applaud the performance of a musician who should play the flute with his nose, or of an artist who should paint with his feet.

My definition of voice may seem to exclude *ventriloquism*. Whatever be the exact method of procedure in the details of that art, it is certain that the sound is always produced *in the larynx*, though it is no doubt modified in various ways by it may not be superfluous to explain the difference between *phonation* and *articulation.* The former is the simple utterance of vocal sound, whilst in the latter the vibrating column of expired air is modified by being broken up into jets or syllables of various kinds. Phonation is, of course, possible without articulation, as in the cries of animals, the screams and cooings of babies, or the yell of the savage; and on the other hand there may be articulation apart from phonation, as in whispering. Some elementary notions of the structure of the parts concerned in these various acts are required for the comprehension of the mode in which the voice is produced, just as, in order to understand the working of a machine, it is necessary to have some acquaintance with the parts of which it is composed.

The organs of voice are threefold in function, and consist of (1) a motor, (2) a vibratory, and (3) a resonant element. The first supplies the air-blast, or *motive power*, the second the *tone*, and the third the *quality* of the voice. To the first group belong the lungs and the windpipe, with the muscles which act upon them; the second consists of the actual organ of voice, *i.e.* the glottis with its vibrating lips; whilst the third comprises several parts above the glottis (ventricles, false cords, epiglottis, pharynx, nose, mouth, bone-cavities of the face, &c.), and one

crowd believe not only that *he* saw the lion over the gateway of old Northumberland House wag its tail, but that *they* also witnessed the phenomenon.

below it, viz. the thorax or chest. These and their mode of action are briefly described in Appendix I., p. 171.

The physiology of the vocal organs is a very difficult subject in itself, and its obscurity has been deepened to almost Cimmerian darkness by the dust and smoke of angry controversy. The sober scientist has shown a remarkable alacrity to rage and imagine vain things; and questions as minute as the *iota* of theology have given rise to terrible heart-burnings among learned professors both of medicine and music—a scientific mixture which has shown an unfortunate proclivity to become incandescent on the slightest provocation. I shall endeavour to walk over the smouldering ashes of these disputes without stirring them up into flame, and shall, therefore, as far as possible avoid questions of mere theory, and confine myself to matters of fact.

It cannot be too clearly understood at the outset that the voice is generated solely *in the larynx.* It is necessary to insist on this elementary fact with some emphasis, so much confusion having been caused by fanciful expressions like "head voice" and "chest voice." Philosophers are never tired of warning us not to mistake *names* for *things*, but it is an error to which we are all liable, and none more so than these estimable persons themselves. The present is a typical example of the danger alluded to.

The originators of the terms "head voice," &c., no doubt applied them with subjective accuracy, *i.e.* the name expressed the fact as they conceived it.

But just as "the evil that men do lives after them," misleading terminology continues to work havoc in the minds of learners long after its falsehood has been recognised by teachers, who, however, adhere to it from a mistaken notion of its practical usefulness. It is no exaggeration to say that most of the confusion in which the whole subject of voice-production is still involved is caused by the use of terms either wrong in themselves or wrongly applied. The larynx is the organ of voice just as the eye is the organ of sight, or the ear of hearing. Every one would laugh at a man who should pretend to smell with his lips or see with his fingers ; yet such claims are not one whit more absurd than those of singers who profess to fetch their voice from the back of the head, the roof of the mouth, the bottom of the chest, or anywhere else that their misinterpreted sensations lead them to fancy. As a *basso profondo* is sometimes figuratively said to "sing out of his boots," we may perhaps be grateful that there is no *voce di piede* among the acknowledged registers.

Before describing what takes place in the larynx whilst the voice is being produced, it will be well to give the reader some idea of how the knowledge which we have on the subject is obtained. Until a short time ago the notions of scientific men as to the working of the organ of voice were derived either from experiments made on the human body after death, or on living animals, or from more or less probable conjectures founded on the analogy of musical instruments of different kinds. Now, however, the inside of the larynx can be seen whilst the parts are at work, and the various movements watched and studied at leisure. The apparatus by which we are enabled to do this is known as the laryngoscope.[1]

This little instrument consists essentially of a small mirror fixed at a somewhat obtuse angle to the end of a slender shank. It is introduced into the mouth, and placed in such a position that the deeper parts of the throat are reflected on its surface where the image can be seen by the observer. The light may fall on the mirror directly from the sun, but as the operator's head is apt to intercept the rays, it is useful to have a second larger mirror on which they may be caught and reflected into the patient's throat in the way familiar enough to mischievous school-

[1] The laryngoscope seems a simple thing, but, like every other improvement, it took a long time to discover, and, as need hardly be added, had to overcome much indifference and scepticism before it was accepted. Then came the usual fierce jealousies as to priority, &c. Like most really valuable additions to medical science, the invention came from an outsider, and this no doubt at first hindered the recognition of its importance. Attempts had been made to see the larynx by Bozzini of Frankfort in the early years of the present century, and after him by Senn of Geneva (1827), Babington of London (1829), Bennati of Paris (1832), Baumês of Lyons (1838), Liston of London (1840), Warden of Edinburgh (1844), and Avery of London (1844). A full account of the instruments devised by these various workers may be found in my little work on the *Use of the Laryngoscope*, 3rd edition, 1871 (Longmans). In 1855 the problem was at last solved by Professor Manuel Garcia, the celebrated *maestro*, who succeeded in seeing his own larynx and watching its movements in respiration, in the formation of vowels, and in singing. Since his results

boys. In our dismal climate, however, the sun can never be relied on as a source of illumination, and even under brighter skies it is often necessary to have an artificial substitute. Much ingenuity worthy of a better cause has been shown in devising elaborate and costly kinds of apparatus to meet the want, but an ordinary lamp giving a fair light is quite sufficient for most purposes. This should be placed on one side of the person to be examined in such a way that the flame is on a level with his eye. The large mirror or "reflector" used by the operator should have a concave surface with a focal power of from twelve to fourteen inches, and it should be perforated in the middle. It should be fixed to the observer's head either by means of a strong spectacle frame or an elastic band, and the aperture in the mirror should be placed opposite his right eye. The patient must then open his mouth wide, and the reflected light from the large or "frontal" mirror must be made to fall on the base

were given to the scientific world, the laryngoscope has come into general use in medicine for the diagnosis and treatment of disease, and the instrument has been perfected in its details. Special mention must be made of my respected teacher, the late Professor Czermak of Pesth, who, besides making improvements of the greatest importance in the apparatus and method of procedure, visited the chief medical centres in Europe as a sort of scientific missionary, demonstrating everywhere the mode of use and practical value of the laryngoscope. But for this it is highly probable that the instrument would have been relegated to the same limbo of oblivion as its predecessors, whilst Garcia's observations would have remained buried in the *Proceedings* of the Royal Society.

of the uvula, *i.e.* its point of attachment to the soft palate. The operator next draws forward the patient's tongue with his left hand, whilst with his right he introduces the small or "laryngeal" mirror, which should be slightly warmed beforehand that it may not be dimmed by the moisture of the breath. It should be lightly held by the handle like a pen, and passed inwards, with the reflecting surface downward, care being taken not to touch either the tongue or the roof of the mouth. When the mirror is seen to be in contact with the upper part of the uvula, it should be made to push the soft palate very gently backwards and a little upwards, when the image of the larynx will appear on the surface. The tendency of beginners is to push the instrument against the back of the throat, a manœuvre which, even if it does not act as an immediate emetic, is sure to bring the attempted examination to an abrupt conclusion. The tongue also is apt to fare badly in the grasp of the "prentice hand," being either squeezed too tightly, or dragged too roughly out of the mouth, or pulled forcibly down so that its under surface is wounded by the lower teeth. The tip of the organ should be lightly held in a small cloth between the thumb and the forefinger, the latter supporting it below so as to protect it from the teeth. The object of pulling the tongue forward is twofold: firstly, to keep it steady and prevent its obstructing the view; and secondly to draw the epiglottis slightly upwards and forwards so that the interior of the larynx can be more easily seen. For purely physiological purposes, however, where it is important to see the parts as much as possible in a state of nature, it is better to make the examination, when practicable, without drawing out the tongue. This unluckily is feasible only in a comparatively small proportion of cases.

On looking into the throat with the laryngoscope the first thing that meets the eye is usually the epiglottis, differing in size and shape in individuals just as much as the nose or any other feature. It is generally curved somewhat upwards and forwards, and thus presents its *under* surface to the observer. Passing backwards from either edge of the epiglottis are two thin red folds, composed of mucous membrane and a few muscular fibres; these help to form the upper rim of the larynx. Behind, they can be seen to join the arytenoid cartilages, the somewhat rounded outline of which, together with the little pea-like cartilages of Santorini and Wrisberg connected with them, can be distinctly seen bulging out at the back. Within the circumference of the outlet, but at a lower level, two pale-red, smooth ledges are visible running from before backwards, and joining the lower part of the arytenoid cartilages. These are the ventricular bands; each of them overhangs a cavity (ventricle of the larynx), of which it forms the upper border. The mouth of the cavity cannot, however, be distinctly seen without slanting the mirror to one side. Deep in the interior of the larynx (*i.e.* in the centre of the image), when it is in a state of repose, the white glistening vocal cords can be seen running in the same direction as the ventricular bands, but nearer the middle line. Sometimes they are not seen until the act of phonation is performed, when each seems to shoot out from under the corresponding ventricular band. The aperture between the vocal cords is wider behind than in front, and forms, as already said, a triangular space (see Fig. 1), the apex of which is at the anterior part where the vocal cords join each other, whilst the base is behind, between the arytenoid cartilages. If the breath is drawn in, as in

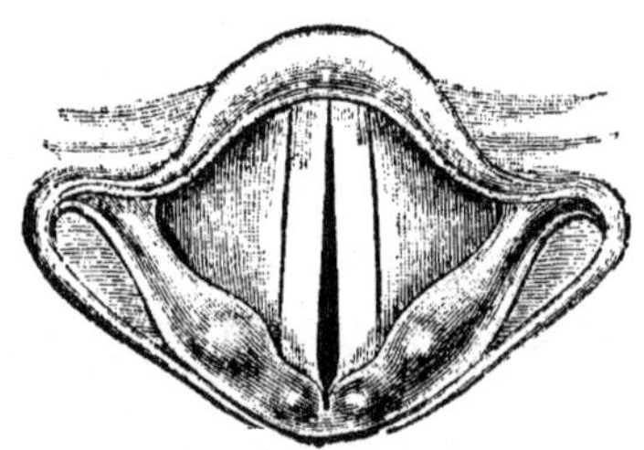

Fig. 1.—The Glottis. (Seen from above during the Emission of a Low Chest Note.)

quiet inspiration, the cords are seen to move a little way apart from each other, and the base of the triangle widens out. If a deep breath is taken, the cords separate still more, and in forced or gasping inspiration they are drawn still more widely apart, affording a glimpse of the inside of the windpipe which in certain cases can be distinctly seen down to the point where it divides into the tubes which go to the lungs. If now the person examined sounds a high note, the hinder part of the glottic orifice, which lies between the inner surface of the two arytenoid cartilages and their anterior "spurs" or "vocal processes" (see Appendix I., p. 179), in other words, the base of the triangle, is seen, as a rule, to close. The remaining portion of the vocal cords is put on the stretch, and the two come together in the middle so as to be in more or less complete apposition throughout their whole length. It must be understood, however, that even when they *touch* each other they are not *pressed close together*, except in the delivery of certain high notes.

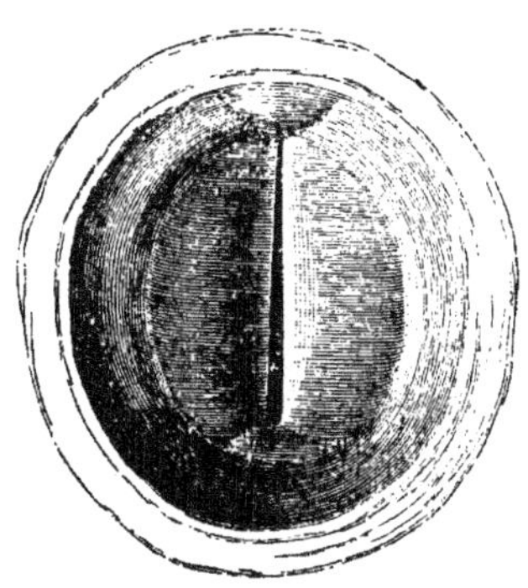

FIG. 2.—THE GLOTTIS. (SEEN FROM BELOW IN AN EXSECTED LARYNX, THE VOCAL CORDS BEING FIXED IN THE POSITION THEY ASSUME IN THE EMISSIO OF A LOW CHEST NOTE IN LIFE.)

N.B.—The projection at the anterior part is the lower edge of the thyroid cartilage, whilst that at the back is the lower edge of the cricoid

In a few rare cases, where the windpipe has been opened below the level of the larynx, it is possible to get a view of the under surface of the vocal cords. It will then be seen that they are not *flat* underneath, but bevelled, so as to form a somewhat conical mouthpiece, so to speak, to the trachea. The accompanying woodcut (Fig. 2) will enable the reader better to realise the formation of the vocal lips.

In studying the laryngoscopic image it must be borne in mind that it is vertical, the parts nearest the mirror appearing highest, and those farthest away occupying the lowest place. The epiglottis, therefore, is seen at the top, and the hinder part of the larynx at the bottom, the vocal cords being visible between the two, and appearing to run upwards to their point of junction below the epiglottis. It must be remembered, too, that the image is reversed as regards the spectator, that is to say, the part which seems most distant from him is in reality nearest, and *vice versâ*, and the cord which corresponds with his right side is the left cord of the person observed, and so on. These complications make laryngoscopy a difficult art to those who have not a practical familiarity with the parts as they are in themselves; no amount of book lore and study of anatomical plates[1] will enable a man to read the writing on the little mirror aright unless it has been supplemented and corrected by the careful examination of an exsected larynx. The difference between the two mental conditions may be compared to that between the knowledge of a district acquired from the study of a railway map and that gained by making an actual survey of the ground.

Laryngoscopic examination is easier in some

[1] It is still more impossible to acquire more than a very hazy notion of the structure or appearance of the larynx from plates alone, in which it is impossible to represent the difference of *level* of the various parts.

persons than in others, and the student should know something of the difficulties that may beset his path. Irritability of the throat is the most common obstacle, the contact of the mirror with the delicate lining membrane causing such distress that the operation cannot be borne. In other persons the tongue arches itself like the back of an angry cat and hides the mirror from view. In others again the epiglottis is doubled over the larynx in such a way that only a small portion of the interior can be seen.

Although the laryngoscope is invaluable in the recog nition and treatment of diseases which before could only be guessed at and let alone, it is surprising how little it has up to the present time added to our knowledge of the *physiology* of the larynx. Indeed, with the exception of certain points relating to the "falsetto" register, the laryngoscope can scarcely be said to have thrown any new light on the mechanism of the voice. This will no doubt be a "hard saying" to many vocalists who look upon the little mirror as a sort of magic glass in which the whole secret of Nature's workmanship is made visible to the eye. A very slight acquaintance with laryngoscopic literature, however, is sufficient to disabuse the mind of any such notion. In speculative subjects one is prepared for any amount of disagreement, but in matters of physical observation a person of even the least sanguine temper might look for a certain degree of uniformity in the results. Instead of this, however, we find *B* upon the direct evidence of his laryngoscope flatly contradicting the statements of *A*, an equally competent observer, whilst *C* again differs from both. No such discrepancy is found in laryngoscopic studies of *disease*; the differences as regards the voice must therefore arise from some special cause. The fact is that much greater skill is required for the examination of the larynx in the act of singing than for ordinary medical purposes, for which in most cases a mere glimpse of the parts is all that is required. Such lightning glances, however, are of little use in elucidating the mysteries of voice-production. The whole of the larynx must lie open to the view; every nook and cranny of its interior must be explored; the most minute change in the relative position of its parts, the least quiver, so to speak, of its muscles must be noted, and all this has to be done for a considerable period of time continuously. It is clear that not only must the observer have a degree of skill altogether beyond the average, but he must be provided with a fairly tolerant subject. His observations must therefore be confined to a comparatively small number of cases, a limitation which must to some extent detract from the value of his results. As a matter of fact hitherto nearly every worker in this field has made his own larynx the principal, if not the sole, object of his attention; the conclusions arrived at under such circumstances can be accepted as valid only for the particular case. The discrepancy between the results in different individuals is perhaps to be explained on that ground. Moreover, the throat can seldom bear such prolonged examination unless it has become hardened to it by repeated practice. For delicate surgical manipulations we find that in most cases a course of *training* is required before they can be undergone. For inspection during singing an even greater degree of tolerance is required. The art of producing the voice with the mirror in the mouth has first to be acquired, and the inside of the larynx must be fully exposed during the whole procedure. The parts must, therefore, be seen under more or less artificial conditions, which may lead the observer utterly astray as to the normal state of things. To avoid these sources of error, as far as possible, investigations should be made on an extensive scale and in a great variety of cases. It is only thus, as a recent writer[1] says, that the "essential" in voice-production can be separated from the "incidental." The classification of Grützner,[2] who divides subjects into three groups, viz. non-singers, natural singers, and trained singers, is unnecessarily exhaustive, for the study of the throat in non-singers can hardly be expected to throw much light on the subject.

In order to get exact views of the larynx the art of photography has been called in to the aid of the laryngeal mirror. Czermak was the pioneer in this as in

[1] Dr. Wesley Mills, "An examination of some controverted points of the physiology of the voice, especially the registers of the singing voice and the falsetto."—*Journal of Physiology*, vol. iv. No. 2.

[2] Physiologie der Stimme und Sprache; *Hermann's Handbuch der Physiologie*, Bd. i. Theil ii. Leipzig, 1879.

other developments of laryngoscopy, but with such indifferent success that he did not feel encouraged to persevere. In 1882 Dr. French and Mr. Brainerd, of Brooklyn, U. S., exhibited to the American Laryngological Association the results of some experiments in the same direction, and soon afterwards Messrs. Browne and Behnke of London published certain mysterious plates, purporting to be photographic studies of the larynx. In some of these a shadowy resemblance to that organ could be traced, with a good deal of help from the imagination, but in others the most experienced anatomist might have been puzzled to say what part of the body he was looking at. In all there was a weird mistiness of outline, irresistibly recalling the attempts of spiritualistic artists to portray the gossamer-like phantoms of our defunct relations. In August, 1884, Dr. French presented to the International Medical Congress at Copenhagen a series of photographs of the larynx of a comparatively high degree of excellence, and the problem may now be considered solved. It is questionable, however, whether the practical outcome of such persevering efforts is at all commensurate with the time and trouble which they must have cost. My own feeling in looking at these photographs is more one of admiration of the ingenuity and resource displayed in overcoming a great difficulty, than of edification by the actual results. No obscure point in the mechanism of the voice has been elucidated by the camera, whilst for purposes of instruction the views of the larynx obtained thereby are less valuable, because less clear, than ordinary drawings.

In examining the larynx of a bass or barytone in the act of singing low notes (when the vibrations are comparatively slow), the vocal cords, and often the arytenoid cartilages can be seen to quiver, the appearance being primarily caused by the *vibration* of the substance of the cords, which is the essential factor of vocal sound. In high notes the vibration is too rapid to be visible, just as the wheels of a railway carriage rotate with such velocity that no movement is perceptible. As a clear conception of vibration is essential for the understanding of the mechanism of the voice, I make no apology for adding a word or two of explanation about it. Vibration is the regular to-and-fro (or in this case, up-and-down) movement, of which there is a familiar exemplification in the pendulum of a clock, or in a tuning-fork when sounding its note. The vibrating body moves through the air for a certain distance, and then returns to its original position. This movement may of course be repeated any number of times, and with greater or less rapidity, every swing this way or that way of the pendulum and every quiver of the tuning-fork being of the same length, and the moving body travelling through an equal distance in an equal space of time. If a body executes such a movement 80 times in a second, the rate of vibration is of course slower than if it were performed 800 times in the same period; the greater or less rapidity of vibration constitutes the fundamental difference in pitch between one tone and another.

Sound is produced by the vibrating body creating a movement in the surrounding atmosphere, just as a stone thrown into water makes ripples on its surface. The particles of the air propagate the impulse one to another, and the *wave* thus formed finally strikes on the ear, making an impression on the

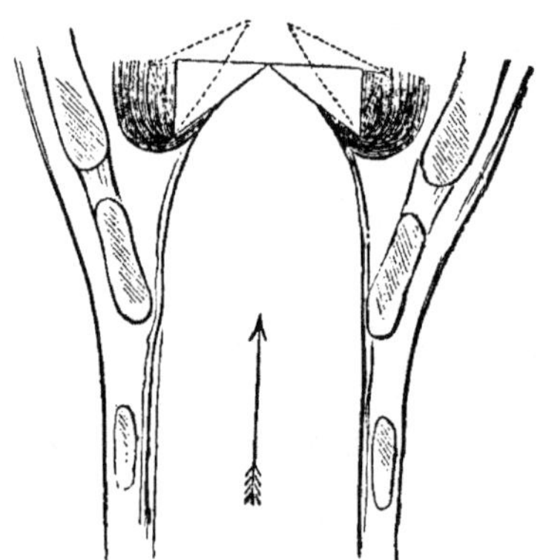

FIG. 3.—THE VOCAL REEDS SHOWN IN A TRANSVERSE VERTICAL SECTION.

The triangular piece near the middle represents the vocal cord proper (the dotted lines showing the course it takes in vibrating); the shaded part to the outer side is the thyro-arytenoid muscle.

auditory nerve which is flashed inwards to the brain, where it is perceived as sound. It follows that there is no sound unless there be a hearer. The thunder rolls in silence, the avalanche falls noiselessly, unless reverberated in a living ear which can translate the rushing of the disturbed atmospheric atoms into sound.

The greater the number of vibrations in a given time, the higher is the tone. If the larynx is watched whilst different notes are being produced, it will be noticed that, whilst the cords are more and more tightly stretched as the voice rises in pitch, they become gradually less and less tense as it descends.

The larynx is a musical instrument, unique in construction, which cannot, strictly speaking, be classed with any other sound-producing apparatus. It bears a close resemblance, however, to the so called *reed* instruments, though differing from them in several important points. Reeds are of different kinds, but the essential feature in all is that they break up a continuous current of air into a series of jets or puffs. Two chief varieties of reed are used in the construction of musical instruments. One consists of a thin plate or "tongue" of metal or wood, one end of which is fixed, whilst the other extremity hangs free in the cavity of a tube, or partly covers an opening after the manner of a valve. The action of such a reed when the loose end or edge is set in motion may be compared to that of a pendulum oscillating about a fixed point. When a blast of air is driven àlong the pipe it strikes the reed, throwing it upwards a certain distance; the tongue then returns, by virtue of its elasticity, to its former position, when it is again pushed up, and so on; in other words, the reed is thrown into *vibration*, and a sound is produced of a pitch corresponding to the length of the vibrating body. The longer the reed the deeper the note, and *vice versâ*. Tongues of this kind may be either single, as in the clarionet, or double, as in the hautboy. Another class of reed consists of plates or disks, which fit into or cover an opening in a tube, without, however, being in actual contact with the edges of the aperture which they close. A familiar example of this arrangement is seen in the tongues of a concertina. The vocal reeds do not resemble either of the kinds just described. They are elastic membranes which must be stretched between their fixed points of attachment before they can be made to vibrate. This is effected by the action of the various muscles acting on the cords; and the degree of tension can be altered and the vibrating element lengthened or shortened at will, so that one cord serves the purpose of many reeds of different sizes, a triumph of economy of material combined with perfection of mechanism to which there is nothing comparable in any musical instrument "made with hands." As there are two vocal cords, it is obvious that the membranous reed in the human larynx is double; in the act of sounding the voice, however, when the cords come together, it is practically a single membrane, with a narrow slit in the centre, stretched from before backwards over the top of the windpipe. An eminent man of science has said that the human eye is so defective as an optical instrument that he would return it to any artificer who sent him so poor a piece of work. I am not aware, however, that this superior person has yet found much evidence of bungling in the larynx, though I have no doubt that, like Alfonso the Wise, if consulted he might have been able to suggest improvements. However that may be, we must be content with the instrument as it is, and even philosophers must allow that the tiny chink with moveable edges can discourse most elcquent music, beyond the power of human inventors to rival.

The *timbre* of the voice is that peculiarity of sound which enables a listener to identify a friend by his voice as readily as he recognises his bodily presence with the eye. Timbre is in fact the physiognomy of the voice. Helmholtz has proposed the somewhat fanciful term *Klangfarbe* ("tone-colour") to replace the word timbre, and Professor Tyndall has translated the word by "clang-tint." Surely there is no need to infringe on the Hibernian monopoly of "bulls" by such a mixture of ideas. To a plain mind the expression "quality of tone" seems to render the notion with perfect adequacy. The various musical instruments have each their own peculiar and characteristic quality of sound; one violin may be discriminated from another by an experienced ear as readily as two different voices. In the case of instruments the difference of tone is no doubt due to their shape and the material of which they are made, and in two of the same class, *e.g.* violins, it is probably dependent on minute differences of form, or on the grain, age, or quality of the wood. In like manner the *timbre* of the voice depends on structural differences in the vocal organs,—size, density, elasticity, and relative situation being no doubt important factors.

Helmholtz[1] has shown that no musical sound is simple, but is in reality composed of a greater or less number of accessory sounds, higher in pitch and fainter in intensity than the fundamental tone, but blending with it so as to supplement it, and, as it were, give it *body*. Each note of the scale has a certain number of these satellites (they are called "harmonics" by musicians) which always accompany it. We know, moreover, that every resonance-chamber has a pitch of its own which responds sympathetically to the vibrations of its proper note, however sounded, and *to no others*. When, therefore, a certain note is uttered, it springs out from the larynx like Minerva from the head of Jupiter, armed *cap-à-pie*, that is with all its harmonics sounding in it. It is obvious that whilst some of these may be in tune with the resonators, others may not; the former, therefore, will be echoed in the pharynx and strengthened, whilst the latter will be more or less drowned. Hence the infinite diversity of voices, no two throats being exactly alike in all their parts. *Timbre* being thus so largely dependent on physical structure may be inherited, and to a certain extent may come to be an ethnological feature. Thus the aborigines of New Zealand, in whom the hollow spaces in the bones of the skull technically called "sinuses," are very ill developed, have voices

[1] "Die Lehre von den Tonempfindungen als physiologische Grundlage fur die Theorie der Musik." Berlin, 1877.

remarkably deficient in resonance. The Italian *ore rotundo* utterance is almost a racial peculiarity; and, if one may say so without impertinence, the voice as well as the speech of our Transatlantic cousins bewrayeth them, just as, it may be presumed, our vocal peculiarities strike their ears.

CHAPTER III.

THE SINGING VOICE.

SECTION I.

The Voice: its Development and Decay.

HULLAH[1] explains the relation of the singing to the speaking voice as consisting in this, that whilst the latter is heard during the passage from one sound to another, *i.e.* at intervals, the former is heard only in "*sounds*—the terms or boundaries of intervals." There is a smack of metaphysical subtlety about this distinction which makes it somewhat difficult to grasp by the ordinary mind. I am almost disposed to doubt whether the difference between speech and song is anything more than that in the former the range is limited to a very few notes delivered without regard to musical time. Song bears the same relation to speech that dancing does to walking; it is the *poetry* of vocal sound. Many speakers utter their sentences with a rhythmical cadence, and even with

[1] *The Cultivation of the Speaking Voice*, 2nd edition, Oxford, 1874, p. 16.

a variety of modulation,[1] approximating to the recitative of the operatic stage. Speech and song, therefore, are as it were the opposite poles of vocal utterance, the interval between them being filled up by *declamation* and *recitative.* The impassioned speech of the ancients was, as Cicero tells us, a *cantus obscurior*, and we read of orators, whose voice was apt to run away with them, taking the precaution of having some one at hand to give them the proper note every now and then with a flute. The difference in most cases between singers and those who have "no voice" is really a defect of *ear* on the part of the latter, who are naturally unable to imitate sounds, that is, reproduce gradations of pitch, which, as a matter of fact, they either do not hear at all, or only imperfectly.

The average compass of the human voice is from two to two and a half octaves; a range of three octaves is exceptional, whilst one of four is almost prodigious. The limits of strength of the voice have not so far as I know been accurately determined; it is obvious that they must depend on circumstances of an almost infinitely variable nature.

The singing voice may begin as early as the age of three; many children can be taught to sing little airs when they are between three and four years old.

[1] Every one who has heard Welsh people talk must have been struck with this. The ordinary speech, too, of the inhabitants of Inverness could no doubt easily be taken down in musical notation by any one with a practised ear.

From the age of six till the period of puberty—fourteen to sixteen—the voice undergoes but little change except in the way of gaining power. A very marked alteration, however, takes place at that time, and this change, though chiefly noticeable in the male sex, is also evident enough in girls. In the former, the voice, after passing through a longer or shorter period of transition, becomes fundamentally altered in character, growing deeper and fuller, and acquiring a "manly" tone. The anatomical features of the change may be summed up as follows:—Increase in size of the larynx in all its dimensions; enlargement and consolidation of the cartilages (thyroid, cricoid, and arytenoid); the angle formed in front by the two wings of the thyroid becomes sharper and more marked, so that it is more prominent in the neck; lastly, the vocal cords become longer and thicker. In the female these physical modifications also take place, though to a much less extent; the voice gains a tone or two in compass, besides becoming stronger, sweeter, and richer. The voice remains much the same throughout adult life, growing fuller, however, up to the age of thirty or even thirty-five, but in men what may be called a second change often occurs between fifty and sixty, or even earlier; the laryngeal cartilages stiffen and turn in part or wholly into bone, whilst the soft tissues lose a portion of their elasticity. In most men after fifty, though sometimes the change is deferred for a year or two, the voice loses power and volume, and often also something in tone, till in extreme old age it becomes shrill and quavering.

> "His big manly voice
> Turning again towards childish treble, pipes
> And whistles in his sound."[1]

In women there is also loss of resonance and flexibility in advanced age, though the change is often scarcely noticeable in ordinary conversation.

It must have been known empirically ever since singing was first cultivated as an art that there are certain points in the ascending scale which it is difficult or impossible for the voice to get beyond without in some way changing the manner of production. The number of these "breaks," as well as the gamut-level at which they occur, varies in individual cases; in nearly all, however, there is one fundamental division between the lower and upper parts of the voice. This is found in most voices at some point which varies in different persons. In other words, at a variable point in the musical scale, there is, as it were, a gulf fixed; on one side of this (the lower) is a series of notes which are produced in a way giving rise to certain sensations; on the other (the higher) is another series

[1] Of course there are exceptional organisations in which the voice retains its freshness and agility even in advanced age. Rubini and Lablache were in "full song" at the age of sixty-two, and Sims Reeves can still produce notes which many a singer in his prime would be glad to possess. Mr. Tom Holmes can yet claim the title of "Champion Tenor" at a period of life considerably beyond the Biblical limit. I may mention, as showing that the retention of the vocal power depends largely on the general organisation, that this gentleman won a cycle race, when he was seventy-six years old, against a most skilful performer in the prime of life.

which can be felt to be delivered in a different manner. The singer is conscious that in order to pass over this gap, either upwards or downwards, his throat instinctively performs some kind of muscular evolution which makes the organs work in a new way. To speak aquatically, there is a sort of natural *lock* whereby the voice can be hoisted up. In this way the *weirs* or "breaks" are avoided, and the voice starts again on a new level. These different vocal *reaches* are technically known as "registers," a word which calls combative professors to battle like a trumpet. In a few persons, however, this double mechanism is not brought into operation, sound flowing on in a regular stream without the necessity for an artificial agency. The wrangling over the registers of the voice has reached almost to the theological degree of heat in certain quarters, and a difference of opinion as to the movements of tiny pieces of gristle and of muscles that to "any thick sight are invisible," or nearly so, has changed the balmy zephyrs of mutual praise into hurricanes of curses.

SECTION II.

The Registers.

It is of the first importance in this somewhat intricate matter to define terms. This is the more necessary as the word "register" has been used in two different senses, one in which it signifies the pitch of a given note, whilst in the other a particular mode of production is meant. By a register I mean *the series of tones of like quality producible by a particular adjustment of the vocal cords.* Strictly speaking, there is a different "register," *i.e.* a certain appropriate condition of the laryngeal orifice for every note, but the actual mechanical principle involved is but twofold. Essentially, then, there are two registers, viz. one (chest) in which the pitch is raised by means of increasing tension and lengthening[1] of the cords as the voice sings upwards; the other (head) in which a similar result is brought about by gradual *shortening* of the vibrating reed, which is still tense, though less so than in the chest register. If, therefore, a new nomenclature is thought necessary to replace the old, the terms "long-reed" and "short-reed" registers would serve well enough to express the two fundamental differences of mechanism in voice-production.[2] Subtle intellects and delicate ears may

> "distinguish and divide
> An inch twixt south and south-west side,"

and quarrel like Hotspur and Glendower as to the limits of the two registers and the apportionment of a given tone to one or the other.[3] It is certain that,

[1] The actual elongation is very slight, not more than a line or so.

[2] The division of "higher" and "lower" used by Mandl and by some of the present teachers of singing in France is objectionable, as many notes can be sung equally well in both registers.

[3] One can scarcely fail to be struck by the fact that whilst nearly all scientific observers, such as Müller, Mandl, Battaille, Vacher, Koch, Meyer, Gouguenheim, and Lermoyez, are content with a twofold division of the voice, musicians (Garcia, Madame Seiler Behnke), affect the more complicated arrangement of five

however over-refining musicians may multiply the "registers" of the voice, *physiologically* there are but two. These fundamental divisions are the so-called "chest" and "head" modes of production, the falsetto mechanism in man corresponding to the head register of the female voice, of which it is in fact an imitation. As the name implies, it is an artificial or "false," in contradistinction to the natural or "chest," voice, just as "false" teeth, however useful and beautiful in themselves, are still not natural.

The long-reed and short-reed mechanisms are the natural features of the vocal territory, all other subdivisions being, as it were, merely political.

The problem may be stated thus: Given a single reed (for the two cords, as has been said, act as one reed), how to produce variety of pitch? Three factors must be taken into account in considering any vocal sound produced by the larynx: first, the degree of tension of the cords; secondly, the quantity of reed that is thrown into vibration (this may vary as regards (*a*) length, and (*b*) breadth); and thirdly, strength of blast. Stretching will of itself raise the pitch, the

registers. There may be a difference of timbre corresponding to each of those divisions, which can be appreciated only by an educated ear, and in the acrobatic larynx of an autolaryngoscopic *maestro* it may be possible for himself to see the minute details of adjustment and vibration which he describes. As to that I can offer no opinion. I do say, however, that in the ordinary human throat not specially trained for self-exhibition, it is not possible to see exactly how much or how little of a vocal cord vibrates, or whether the apposition of the arytenoids is of such a nature as to close the cartilaginous glottis hermetically or not.

strength of blast remaining the same, and conversely increase of blowing-power alone will heighten pitch, the tension remaining the same. There are limits, of course, beyond which neither the tension nor the air-blast can be increased. The difficulty is met by shortening the cords, *i.e.* providing a shorter reed, whereby, *ipso facto*, pitch is raised, and can be heightened still more with less expenditure of wind-power. In putting forward this view I make no claim to originality. The reed theory of the voice has been almost universally accepted for many years. Since Magendie[1] propounded it, Müller's experiments have established its truth. The former physiologist even went so far as to say, that, in dogs at least, as the notes become more acute the reed is gradually shortened.[2] The only novelty which I have ventured to put forward is that the essential factor in chest-production is the long reed, whilst the essential factor in the head-delivery is the short reed. I do not wish this theory to be considered a master-key which will unlock every mysterious recess of the subject. I merely offer it as what may be called the solid residue after the various theories have been submitted to the flame of criticism, and their gaseous elements (which are largely in excess) dissipated.

[1] *Précis Élémentaire de Physiologie*, 3rd edition, Paris, 1833 t. i. p. 292 *et seq.*

[2] It is curious that in dogs the shortening of the reed takes place progressively *from the front.*—Magendie, *op. cit.* p. 302.

On looking into the larynx during singing, the position of the vocal reed, *i.e.* the two vocal cords acting together, can be seen, and the form and size of the orifice through which air passes upwards can also be observed. The difficulties in the way of an adequate examination are so great that to obtain a complete view of the whole process a very large number of singers have to be examined. Thus in order to study the working of the vocal cords throughout the *entire scale* in fifty persons, I found it necessary to examine between three and four hundred singers. It has been judiciously observed that in order to study the action of the vocal cords in singing, a large number of practised vocalists should be examined by an expert laryngoscopist.[1] Concurring in this view I have looked only at the throats of persons gifted with fine voices. My cases include a great many of the best singers of the day; of the fifty, forty-two were trained, whilst eight were natural singers: I have not included any "non-singers," for, as already said, I did not consider they would be of any use for the purpose in view. Before describing my own observations, I must remind the reader who is not familiar with anatomical details, first, that the space between the vocal cords is called the glottis or glottic chink (see Figs. 4 and 5 *og* and *og'*); secondly, that the vocal sounds are produced by the vibration of the free edges or lips of the

[1] Gordon Holmes: *Vocal Physiology and Hygiene*, 2nd edition, p. 118, footnote.

glottis, *i e.* of the reeds commonly called the "vocal cords"; thirdly, that the anterior three-quarters of these lips consist of ligamentous or elastic tissue

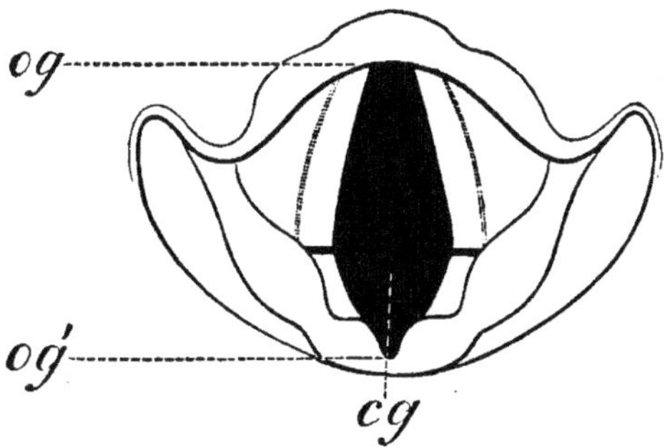

FIG. 4.—DIAGRAM SHOWING THE GLOTTIS IN DEEP INSPIRATION.
og, *og'*, orifice of the glottis: the space in front of (above) the small cross lines is the ligamentous glottis; that behind (below) them, or *cg*, is the cartilaginous glottis.

whilst the posterior fourth is formed of gristle, being in fact the base of the arytenoid cartilage (see Figs. 2 and 3). Hence this opening is divided into

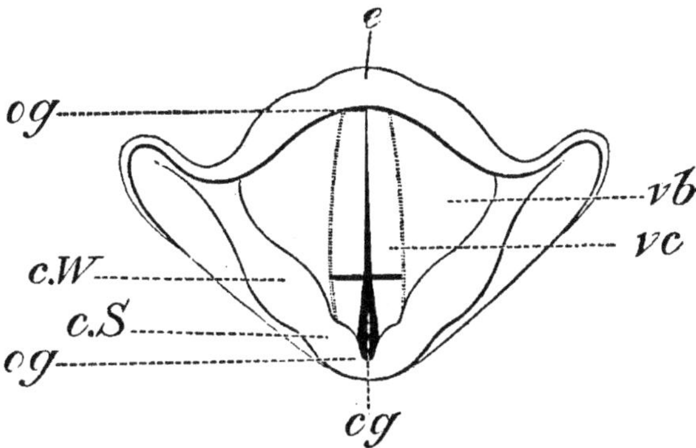

FIG. 5.—DIAGRAM SHOWING THE GLOTTIS IN PHONATION. THE PART BELOW (BEHIND) THE CROSS LINE IS THE CARTILAGINOUS GLOTTIS.
e, epiglottis; *og*, *og'*, orifice of the glottis; *cg*, cartilaginous glottis; *vb*, ventricular band; *vc*, vocal cord; *c.W*, cartilage of Wrisberg; *c.S*, capitulum Santorini.
(For further explanations as to the relative positions of the ligamentous glottis and the cartilaginous glottis, see Fig. 4.)

the ligamentous glottis and the cartilaginous glottis, the vocal process or anterior spurs of the arytenoid cartilage constituting the line of separation. Only the anterior or ligamentous portion forms the true reed. Speaking generally, it may be said that the cartilaginous glottis is generally open in the lower,

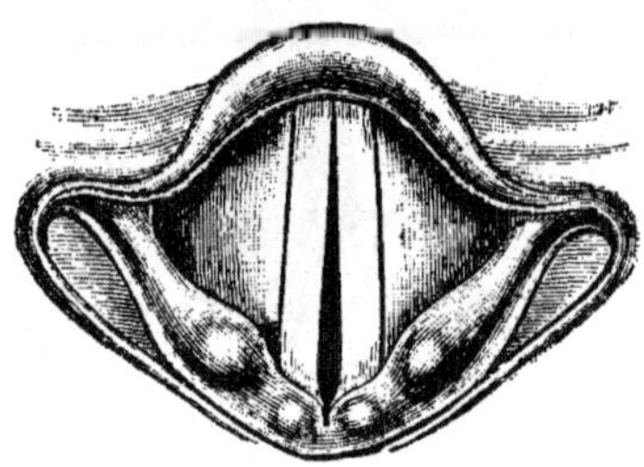

Fig. 6.—Laryngoscopic View of the Male Glottis in the Delivery of a Low Note.

and gently closed in the upper notes of the chest, and that a segment of the ligamentous glottis is *tightly* closed in the head voice.

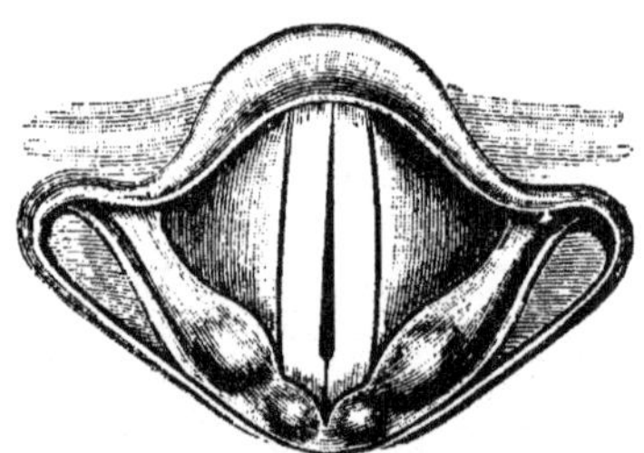

Fig. 7.—Laryngoscopic View of the Male Glottis in the Delivery of a High Note.

Entering into greater detail respecting my cases (see Appendix), the following observations were made. First, that in tenor voices the whole glottis is open to

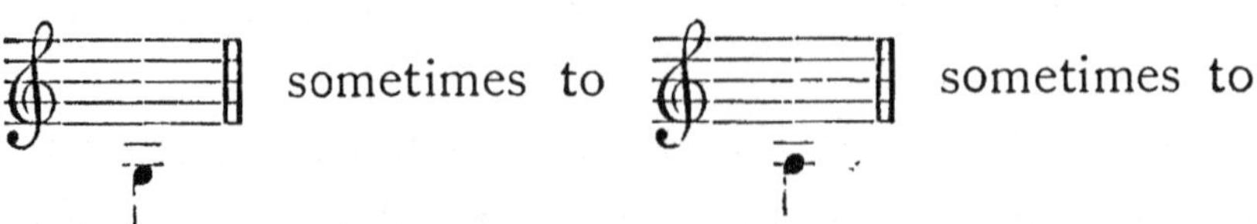

sometimes to sometimes to

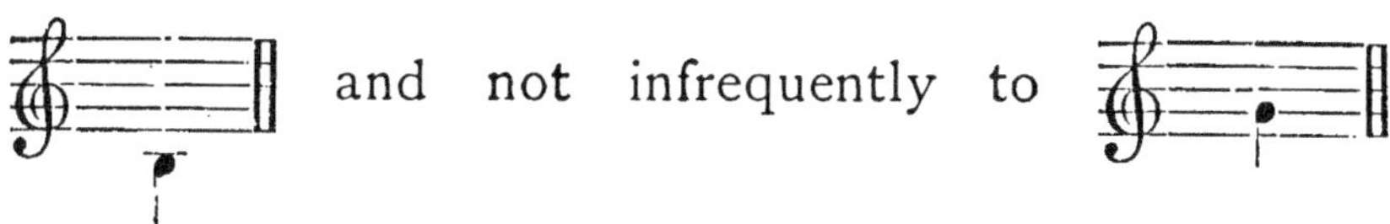
and not infrequently to

Beyond this note, closure of the cartilaginous portion of the glottis takes place. Sometimes, on the other hand, the whole glottis is open throughout. Secondly, that in barytone voices the whole glottis is often open to

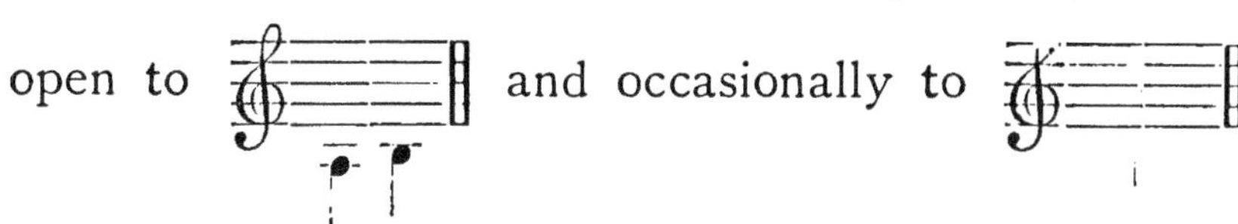
and occasionally to

Beyond this note the cartilaginous portion of the glottis is closed, except in the rare cases in which the entire glottis remains open. Thirdly, that in the bass voice the whole glottis is sometimes open to

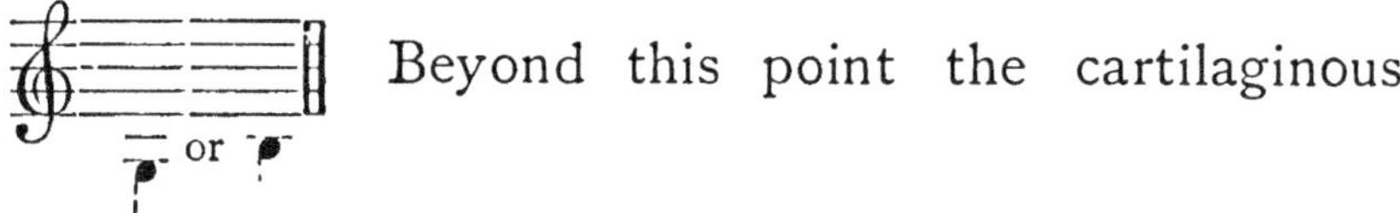

Beyond this point the cartilaginous glottis is gradually closed, except in the few instances in which the whole glottis remains open. Fourthly, that in sopranos and mezzo-sopranos the whole glottis is sometimes open to

often to

beyond which the cartilaginous glottis is usually closed. The glottis is sometimes closed throughout the scale, and in one case it was open throughout. Fifthly, that in contralto voices the whole glottis is often open to

Beyond this the carti-

laginous portion is closed. Sixthly, that in the head voice of women and the falsetto of men, stop-closure (see page 41) always takes place in the posterior

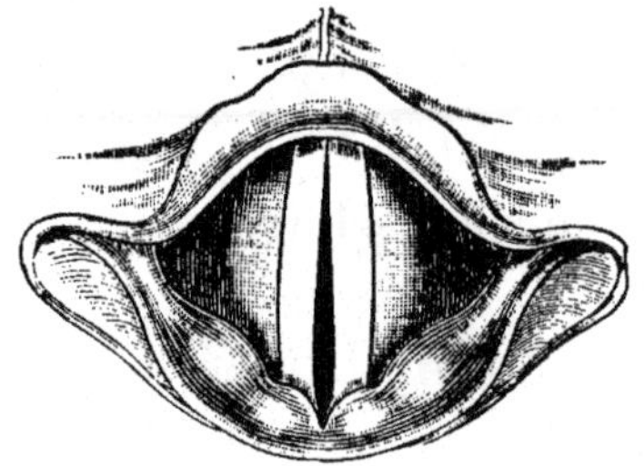

Fig. 8.—Laryngoscopic View of the Female Glottis in the Production of a Low Note.

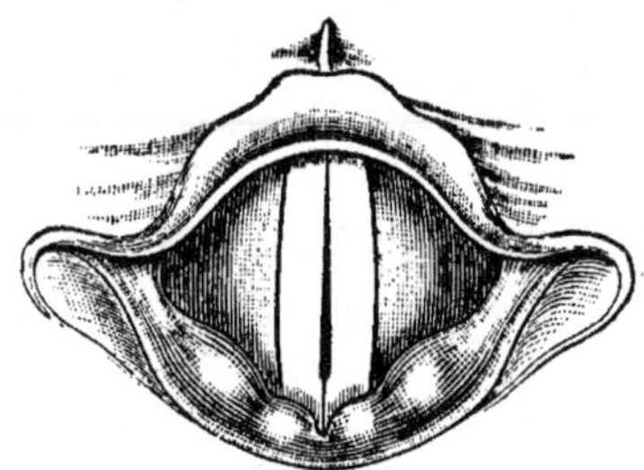

Fig. 9.—Laryngoscopic View of the Female Glottis in the Production of a High Note (Long Reed).

portion of the ligamentous glottis and sometimes at the anterior part also. In the former cases there is an elliptical opening extending to the anterior commissure of the vocal cords; in the latter the elliptical

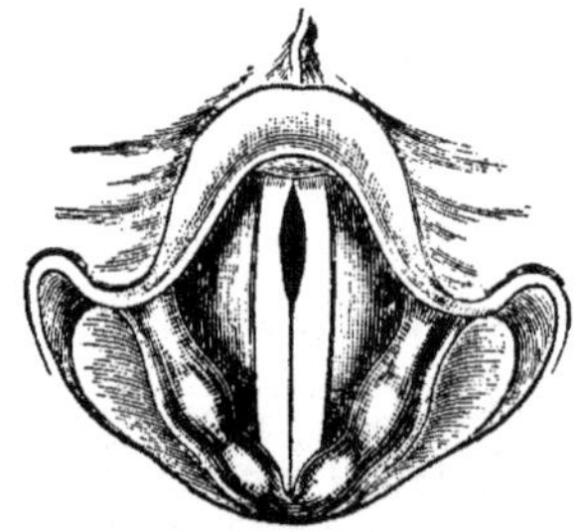

Fig. 10.—Laryngoscopic View of the Female Glottis in the Delivery of a Head-note (Ordinary appearance).

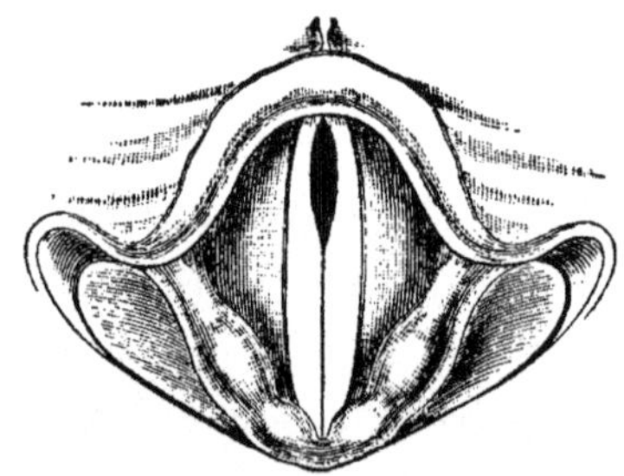

Fig. 11.—Laryngoscopic View of the Male Glottis in Falsetto Singing (Ordinary appearance).

opening occupies the middle third of the ligamentous glottis.

The closure of the posterior part of the glottis does not seem to be a very important matter, as it does not affect the vibratory element, and it is highly probable that some air passes up through the hinder portion during singing even when apparent closure has taken place. There is another kind of closure, however, which is much more significant, and that is "stop-closure." By this term I understand a condition of the glottis in which its membranous lips are not simply in contact, but pressed together so tightly for a greater or less portion of their length as to prevent each other from vibrating at that part. This is done either by the edge of one lip overlapping that of the other, or by both cords being forced against each other in such a way as to turn their edges upwards. This mechanism is brought into use whenever the head-notes are employed by women or the falsetto by men. In this condition the back part of the interval between the vocal cords themselves is not merely closed but the two cords are tightly pressed against each other for a certain length; in the portion where they "jam" in this way all vibration is stopped, and thus the long reed is converted into a short reed. Sometimes the vocal cords are also pressed together anteriorly. This latter condition has been looked upon by many observers as the usual one, but I have found simple posterior stop-closure the most common. Whether the stop action occurs only behind, or both behind and in front, the elliptical opening between the lips of the glottis invariably becomes progressively shorter (from behind forwards) as the voice rises. In only two cases have I seen any exception, and in these the elliptical opening was formed at the back of the glottis just in front of the vocal process. This was noticed once in the larynx of a good singer, whose case is included in the table in Appendix III. In the other instance the centre of the elliptical opening corresponded with the vocal process. The subject was a music-hall singer, who called his performance "descriptive." This case is not included in

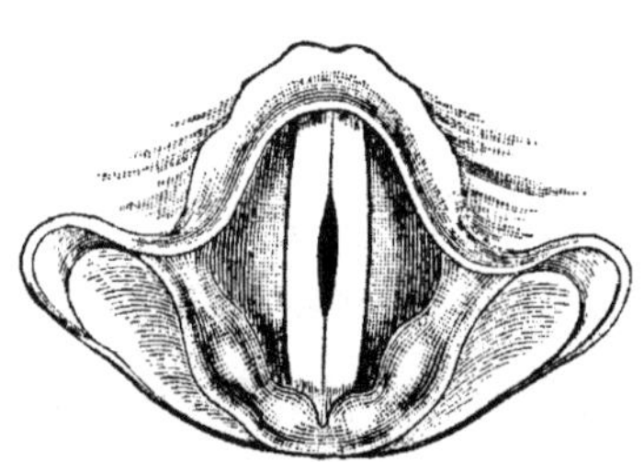

Fig. 12.—Laryngoscopic View of Female Glottis in Head Register (Exceptional Type, though generally described as the Common one).

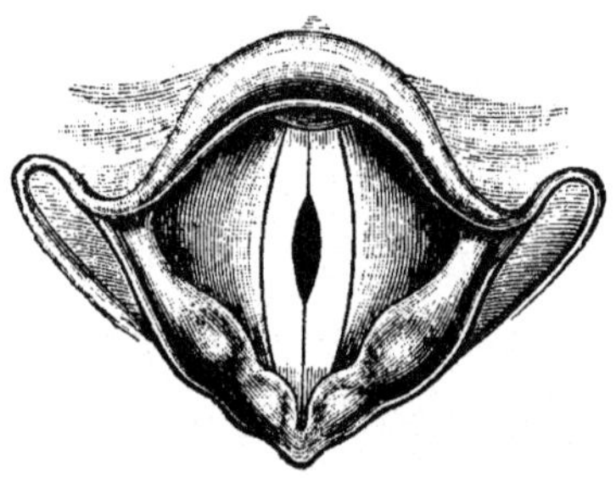

Fig. 13.—Laryngoscopic View of the Male Glottis in the Falsetto Production (Exceptional Type, though generally described as the Common one).

my table. After the stop action has occurred and sometimes before, the posterior part of the glottis is covered by the close apposition of the arytenoid cartilages and *capitula Santorini.* Cases in which the covering process takes place *before* stop-closure have been excluded from my table (see Appendix III.). The long reed (chest voice) is generally used by pure sopranos. Figs. 8 and 9 show the action of the vocal cords in the case of Madame Nilsson, Madame Albani, and Madame Valleria.[1] On the other hand, contralto singers sing their high notes almost invariably in the head register (or short reed): this mechanism of the high notes is shown in the case of Madame Patey and several other fine contralto singers in Fig. 10. Mezzo-sopranos also generally make use of both the long and short reed. Most tenors use both reeds, five-sixths of the notes being sung with the long reed, the remainder with the short reed, but a few confine themselves entirely to the long reed. On the other hand, one of the most charming ballad singers of the day employs the short reed in the production of the upper three-fourths of his voice. Barytones whilst keeping within their proper compass use the long reed, and bass singers confine themselves entirely to this mechanism. The finest alto singers amongst men spring from bass or barytone singers who use the falsetto or short reed, but the *exclusive* use of the falsetto by these singers ultimately destroys the natural register or long reed. If both registers are constantly exercised no harm is done. Mr. Corney Grain is able to sing two octaves with the long reed, and one higher one with the short reed, *i.e.* in falsetto, and it is difficult to tell which register is the finer.

That the falsetto is really an *artificial* mode of

[1] Mancini (*Pensieri e riflessioni pratiche sopra il canto figurato*, Vienna, 1774, p. 43) says that in certain rare instances there is only one register—the "chest"—throughout the whole compass of the voice:—"Si da anche qualche raro esempio che qualcheduno riceve dalla natura il singolarissimo dono di poter eseguir tutto colla sola voce di petto."

voice-production is shown by the fact that young adults who are "natural singers" never use it. In fact, there is a strong impression in unsophisticated minds that the falsetto is a kind of "dodge," to which it is not fair to resort. This idea is probably founded on the fact that the untrained falsetto is usually so poor and disagreeable in quality.

Before the development of the larynx at puberty the long reed is still relatively short, and from an examination of a great number of cases, I am able to affirm that boys who sing alto always use the chest register. Although the peculiar timbre of the voice generally makes it evident which register is being employed, this is not always the case. Thus Mr. Lely's voice has much of the character of the short reed, but the mechanism used is entirely that of the long reed. Again, many of the beautiful notes in Miss Florence St. John's voice have the head tone, but nevertheless the whole of the voice is produced with the chest register.

Returning to the mechanism of the falsetto some further observations must be made. It is generally believed that in the falsetto the vocal cords are relaxed, and that only their margins vibrate. It must be clearly understood that the relaxation is only *comparative;* the cords require to have a certain degree of tension to vibrate at all, but it is proportionately less in the falsetto than in the chest register in order to compensate for the diminished strength of blast in the former. The sense of relief which is experienced in passing from the long to the short reed is probably due to this cause and also in some measure to the increase in the size of the opening between the vocal cords, freer exit of air being thus permitted. As regards the theory of marginal vibration, it may be remarked that it owes its origin to a single experiment of Lehfeldt (see Appendix II., p. 197) which, in blowing air up the trachea, he produced in an exsected larynx a sound somewhat resembling that of the flageolet. On looking at the vocal cords with a magnifying glass, he thought that the margins and not the whole substance of the vocal cords vibrated. Accepted by Müller, this theory has come to be regarded as almost an ultimate fact in the physiology of voice-production. All, however, that is seen with the laryngoscope is that in the head and falsetto registers there is an elliptical opening between the vocal cords near their anterior commissure.

Although Lehfeldt could recognise the limitation of the vibrations on an exsected larynx entirely under his control only with the aid of a lens, many laryngoscopists have gone so far as to say that they have been able to see these vibrations in the laryngeal mirror. It is difficult, however, to imagine that such limited movements could be visible with the naked eye at a distance of twelve inches (the nearest point at which it is possible to obtain a good view of the larynx) when it is remembered that the parts of which the vibrations are said to be seen do not exceed half an inch in length and a sixteenth of an inch in width. It is still more incredible that the keenest sight could perceive that one portion of so small and distant an object vibrates whilst another remains fixed ; yet we are asked to believe that it could be *seen* that "the fine edges of the vocal cords were alone vibrating"! It should be borne in mind also that these vibrations may take place at a rate of nearly 1,000 per second, or, if we include both the to-and-fro movements of vibration, as is the custom in France, at the rate of nearly 2,000 *per second!* Furthermore the vibrations are primarily up and down (not from side to side), the observer looking on the upper surface of the cords, and therefore being in a position in which the difficulty of noticing such movements is greatly intensified. I must confess that I have never myself been able to see such vibrations in high notes, whether chest or falsetto ; I have only been able to see them in the lower notes, especially in barytone and bass singers, and in the production of the speaking voice.

The mechanism by which the outer portion of the vocal cords is prevented from vibrating is generally supposed to be the contraction of the lateral fibres of the thyro-arytenoid muscle (see Appendix I., p. 180), but according to Mandl a further vibration-checking apparatus is supplied in the falsetto by the ventricular bands which are forcibly drawn down so as to press on the upper surface of the vocal cord, and by that means leave only a narrow free margin to be acted on by the air-blast. However plausible this may be as a theory, it is, as Holmes points out, difficult if not impossible to establish by direct observation, as the parts cannot be looked at obliquely enough to determine whether there is actual contact of the ventricular bands with the cords. Though I have often tried to see the action, I have never succeeded. Nevertheless it is right to state that MM. Gouguenheim and Lermoyez say they have seen it in one case, a bass singer in the act of using the falsetto register.[1] Madame Seiler thinks that the anterior closure of the vocal cords is often facilitated by the presence of minute pieces of cartilage in the substance of the cord in this situation. She suggests that they may be more often present in the female than in the male larynx, and as, from its larger size, the latter is generally made use of for dissection, they may have thus been overlooked by anatomists. Madame Seiler states that her observations are supported by the description in Wilson's Anatomy, but, as far as I have been able to ascertain, the small cartilages referred to in that text-book are situated between the cartilages of Wrisberg and Santorini. Dr. Elsberg, however, appears to have met with cartilages corresponding to those described by Madame Seiler. I have seen with the laryngoscope four cases in which small white flecks were present in the anterior part of the vocal cords. They did not cause any projection, and may have been of cartilaginous structure, but in every one of these

[1] *Physiologie de la Voix et du Chant*, p. 142, Paris, 1885.

instances the individual concerned sang out of tune. The subjects were all women, and in none did any benefit arise from treatment. I have on several occasions examined dissected female larynxes with the express object of discovering the cartilages described by Madame Seiler, but I have not been so fortunate as to meet with them.

As regards the action of the parts above the glottis, it is admitted by all that in the lowest tones of the voice the epiglottis falls back over the larynx so as to leave little more than the arytenoid cartilages visible. As the pitch rises so does the epiglottis, and when the upper falsetto or head register is reached the whole length of the cords becomes exposed to view. Garcia[1] goes so far as to make a widely open condition of the upper outlet of the larynx a distinguishing feature of falsetto production. Holmes, on the other hand, maintains that in the production of falsetto "the rim of the larynx instead of becoming dilated suffers a progressive and marked constriction until at last only the edges of the vocal bands can be seen through the narrow orifice that remains."[2] My own investigations are entirely in accordance with these observations of Holmes. In other words, the sound produced in the glottis is as it were *squeezed* through an inverted funnel as it passes upwards into the mouth. A somewhat similar action

[1] *Observations Physiologiques sur la Voix Humaine*, 2nd ed., Paris, 1861.

[2] *Op. cit.* p. 119.

is believed by others to take place in the pharynx (see Appendix I. p. 187), the walls of which, as already said, are muscular, and Mills attributes to this cause the sense of fatigue in that region which is often experienced in production of the head voice.[1]

MM. Gouguenheim and Lermoyez[2] attach much importance to the fact that in the falsetto register the soft palate is forcibly drawn back and upwards so as entirely to prevent the passage of air through the nose. Experimental proof of this is, according to them, afforded by the fact that if the vowel *e* (pronounced like our English *a* as in *fate*) be uttered in a chest tone whilst the nostrils are compressed it has a distinctly nasal character, whereas if sounded in the head register, under the same conditions, the nasal twang is absent, whence it may be inferred that in the latter case the whole of the air-current passes through the mouth.

There are other movements which take place in the head register, and which also occur, though to a much more limited extent, in the high notes of the chest voice. Thus, as the soft palate rises more and more, traction is necessarily made on its pillars (see Appendix I. p. 190), which are attached to the sides of the throat near the back of the tongue. Now these ridges or pillars are in reality bundles of muscular fibres, one of which (the anterior) is attached to the tongue, whilst the other is directly connected with the upper cartilage (thyroid) of the

[1] *Loc. cit.* p. 153.

[2] *Op. cit.* p. 157.

larynx. Elevation of the soft palate must therefore *ipso facto* tend to pull up the tongue and the larynx, an action which is assisted by the sympathetic contraction of the muscular pillars themselves. This is how it is that the larynx, as may be verified by any one for himself, rises in the throat as the voice goes higher, a change of position which some writers have regarded as an essential feature in the production of head tones. That it is not so is proved by the fact that falsetto notes can be sounded without any accompanying elevation of the larynx, provided that the tongue be fixed. The larynx certainly moves a little downward towards the chest in the utterance of deep notes; this, however, is a consequence rather than a cause of low pitch, as the singer instinctively relaxes all the muscles supporting the organ so that the cords may be in the position of least tension. The lowering of the chin towards the breast-bone is part of the same natural adjustment. The reverse of this action is seen in tenors and sopranos when the head is thrown back in the delivery of high head notes. The whole distance which the larynx traverses from the deepest chest to the highest falsetto tone is so inconsiderable (not much more than half an inch) that the mere lengthening or shortening of the vocal tube within so limited a range can hardly have much effect on the pitch of the sound produced. The elevation of the larynx just spoken of must not be confounded with approximation of the cricoid and thyroid cartilages and consequent obliteration of the interval between their borders in front (crico-thyroid space, see Fig. 15). This latter movement in no way affects the position of the larynx as a whole, but only the condition of the vocal cords in respect of antero-posterior tension. Approximation of the cartilages stretches, whilst separation of them relaxes, the vocal cords. Accordingly we find that at the lowest part of the chest register the interval is at its widest, whereas in the upper the gap entirely disappears, as can easily be verified by the singer's own finger.

It is probable that the two wings (see Appendix I. p. 177) of the thyroid are drawn apart to some extent in the lower notes and pressed together in the upper. A vertical notch extends some way down in front between these wings, and this feature is much more pronounced in men than in women. It is obvious that this formation must make the two sides of the cartilage more moveable, *i.e.* that owing to its presence they can be pulled further apart Teleologists would say that this fact shows the purpose of the notch, the male voice requiring a wider glottis for its deep full tones than the shriller female.

With respect to the parts below the glottis, the trachea rises to a slight extent out of the chest as the voice goes upwards. This, however, has probably little or no effect either on the pitch or quality of the note, but is merely the mechanical result of increased breath-power, the larynx being in fact blown upwards by the air-current, and pulling the wind-pipe up with it. In the chest itself there is this notable difference in the two registers, that whereas in the lower the thoracic walls shake strongly, as can be felt on applying the hand to the singer's chest (hence the term *chest* notes), the vibration becomes gradually fainter as the higher notes are reached, finally ceasing altogether in the falsetto.

Reviewing the whole question, it cannot be denied that the subject is beset with difficulties. Four means of investigation have been employed in the acquisition of such knowledge as we possess about the production of the voice: (1) Subjective sensation; (2) analogy; (3) experiment; (4) direct observation. Whilst some of these methods are simply fallacious, none of them is entirely satisfactory. It is reasoning from mere sensation that has given rise to the terms "head," "falsetto," &c., and opened the way to all sorts of absurd notions as to the site and manner of vocal production. Thus whilst one singer will maintain that he makes his falsetto notes at the back of his nose, another professes to fetch them from the top of his skull, and each adduces the evidence of his own consciousness as positively as Goldsmith did when he argued that he moved his *upper* jaw in eating. Sensation which is always an untrustworthy interpreter in all that relates to the workings of our internal economy is particularly treacherous in regard to the throat. I have almost daily occasion to observe this in patients who localise with the nicest precision an uncomfortable feeling, the true cause of which is *visibly* somewhere else. It is often almost impossible to convince a person that a bone or other foreign substance which may have stuck in his throat has been removed even when he is shown the *corpus delicti.* Sensation, however, is a useful witness in confirming the results arrived at in other ways, and it can always be relied on when it tells whether an action causes strain or not. The conclusions reached as to the voice by reasoning from analogy have already been incidentally touched on in speaking of the musical instruments to which it has been compared. Analogy serves very well for illustration, but is always an unsafe foundation on which to rest a theory. With the exception of the drum and the triangle there is scarcely an instrument which has not been found to present a striking resemblance to the human organ of voice. It has so far also escaped being compared to the bagpipe, but the ventricles offer too tempting a likeness to the "drone" for the similarity to remain long unperceived! The beginning of wisdom in studying the voice is to clear the mind of all pre-conceived ideas as to its resemblance to this or that instrument, and study it by itself in the light of anatomical and physical science. It cannot be too strongly affirmed that the human larynx is an instrument absolutely *sui generis.* There can be no doubt that the perverse ingenuity of analogical fancy in this matter has had a retarding influence on our knowledge of voice-production.

Experiment is so difficult of application that its range of usefulness is necessarily limited. Müller's results are open to the objection that the conditions of vocal utterance in the separated larynx are altogether different from those in the living throat. His observations were made, so to speak, on the *skeleton* of the voice, but as far as they go they afford valuable help in disentangling the complex elements of the vocal function. The experiments which have been made on the living larynx have almost all been made on animals. It need hardly be pointed out that no conclusive evidence about the mode of production of the human voice can be drawn from that of brutes.

Direct observation with the laryngoscope is of course the best method at our disposal, but that even its testimony is far from unexceptionable is obvious from the marvellous differences as to matters of *fact* that exist amongst observers. It is hardly too much to say that no two of them quite agree as to what is seen, and the feuds are as bitter as the famous one about the two sides of the shield. The observations which have been made hitherto have for the most part been confined to a few trained throats, and in many cases the examinations have been almost entirely auto-laryngoscopic.

*** *The subject of the registers, and the various views on this difficult problem, have been further discussed in Appendix II.,* *p.* 193. *It is hoped that in the above Section the matter has been made sufficiently clear to the general reader and to the ordinary student of singing.*

CHAPTER IV.

TRAINING OF THE SINGING VOICE.

SECTION I.

The Selection of a Singing Master.

BEARING in mind the reproof addressed to the cobbler-connoisseur of old, I will not in my remarks on the cultivation of the voice touch on the æsthetic side of the subject. I may, however, as a physician who has been constantly seeing the throats of singers of every rank in the musical hierarchy for nearly a quarter of a century, be allowed to express an opinion on the physical effects of voice training.

The object aimed at is twofold. First, the development of the powers of the vocal organs to the fullest extent, and secondly, the education of the voice as an instrument of artistic expression. With the latter I have no direct concern, except in as far as inartistic delivery is also wrong physiologically. The rules of voice-production are not arbitrary canons invented of malice aforethought by musical teachers, and varying according to individual taste or whim They are rational laws founded on the observation of natural processes, and drawn from the practice of the best singers, just as the rules of grammar are the generalised formulæ of the purest speech. They are not by any means intended to "correct" Nature or bring her ways into conformity with fantastic standards existing in the minds of crotchety *maestri*, and cherished by them as if they were the very "archetypal ideas" of the Divine Intelligence. With every allowance for the hyperbolical forms in which the artistic temperament finds its natural expression, the boast heard on the lips of some singing-masters that they can *create* a voice is as absurd as it is arrogant. Does the trainer put fleetness into the legs of the racehorse, or give strength to the arm of the pugilist? The function of the teacher is important enough without any such ridiculous pretensions, for without him the natural endowment would fall short of its proper measure of achievement. Untrained talent is like learning unquickened by wine, according to Falstaff, "a mere hoard of gold kept by a devil till sack sets it in act and use." Singers indeed there are who trust to natural faculty alone, and deem themselves above rules, as a certain emperor declared himself to be *supra grammaticam*. Many persons are apt to be misled into a thoughtless admiration of untutored geniuses by a preference which they fancy themselves to have for "nature" as compared with "art." But true art is in this case perfected nature, and the supposed antithesis is altogether imaginary. However richly gifted by nature a singer may be, he must be taught how to put forth his powers to the best purpose, and how to husband them that they may not fall into premature decay. In fact, the better the voice the more need there is for its being trained to its full degree of excellence that its artistic destiny may be fulfilled and the world may not be made poorer by its untimely loss.

It is most desirable that the voice should as far as possible be properly trained from the very first so that at any rate there may be nothing to unlearn. Afterwards, when the real education commences, it is of the utmost importance to have a thoroughly good teacher. But how, it may be asked, in such a crowd of pretenders are competent instructors to be distinguished from quacks? I answer (not to speak it profanely), "By their fruits ye shall know them." As a doctor is judged by the proportion of cures which he effects, and an advocate by the number of rogues he saves from hanging, the ability of a singing-master is measured by the excellence of his pupils. Do they sing well? and do their voices last? This practical test is the only sure criterion, and it is not an unfair one, if applied with proper discriminal tion. That is to say, the aggregate results ought to be taken into account, not merely stray cases here and there of exceptional merit or the reverse. It would be nothing to the purpose for an unsuccessful teacher to attribute his failure to want of aptitude on the part of his pupils, for it is just in poor organisations that a sound method of instruction achieves its greatest triumphs. Agriculture is nowhere seen in higher perfection than in Scotland, where the soil is naturally very barren. The ideal singing-master, if we are to believe certain professors of the art, is a monster of all-round perfection, as impossible to find *in rerum naturâ* as Rasselas's poet, or Macaulay's omniscient schoolboy. But as a matter of fact the endowments and acquirements needed are rare and manifold enough to make it needless to exaggerate them. It is not every one who can sing, or who knows what good singing is, that is fit to teach the art. In addition to the qualifications which all true instructors should possess—thorough knowledge of the subject, wide experience, sound judgment, clearness of thought and expression, sympathetic insight, personal enthusiasm and the power of kindling it in others, combined with the patience of Job and the energy of Hercules,—the singing-master must have, of course, the special qualities of his craft. The question is often debated whether the master should himself be a singer or not. Teachers naturally argue the question from the standpoint of their own personal gifts. At first sight one is disposed to say that a singing-master who cannot sing is like the dancing-master spoken of by Swift, who had every good quality except that he was *lame*. This view, however, is really a fallacy akin to "Who drives fat oxen must himself be fat." A singing-master must be able to sing at least well enough to exemplify his own precepts, and show his pupils *how* to produce the voice and how *not.* He need not, however, be a brilliant performer; indeed, I believe several of the most successful voice-trainers of the day have themselves little or none of the divine gift which they cultivate in others. The greatest practical adepts in any art are not by any means always the best teachers of it, not merely from lack of the necessary patience, but from want of the power of imparting knowledge. The hone, which, although it cannot cut, can sharpen the razor; the finger-post that shows the way which itself can never go, are emblems of the teacher.[1]

[1] Tosi (*op. cit.* p. 8), with some bitterness, advises any one wishing to undertake the work of teaching to "read, mark, and inwardly digest" Virgil's well-known challenge-lines:—

> "*Sic vos non vobis vellera fertis oves!*
> *Sic vos non vobis nidificatis aves!*
> *Sic vos non vobis mellificatis apes!*
> *Sic vos non vobis fertis aratra boves!*"

which may be "freely Englished," or rather "adapted," as follows:—

> "Not for herself the cow doth store her milk,
> Not for itself the worm doth weave its silk;
> Not for itself its pearl the oyster bears,
> Not for itself its coat the ermine wears;
> Not for himself the jackal stalks the prey,
> Not for himself the poor "ghost" moulds the clay:
> The soldier fights—the captain gets the spoils,
> And for his pupil's fame the teacher toils."

It cannot be pleasant, as Tosi says, "*a chi ha sete di portar il vino agli altri e non poter bere.*"

This may at first sight seem to be a very humble function, but it must be borne in mind that the instruction of others is as much an art *sui generis* as that of singing itself, and it is only by a fortunate coincidence that the capacity for both may sometimes be found in the same individual.[1] No doubt, however, for public singing the guidance of one who has himself gone successfully through the ordeal, has the priceless value which attaches to practical experience.

If a maestro may be allowed to have an indifferent voice, he must, on the other hand, possess an ear of the nicest precision. He should also have a refined catholicity of taste, fed on the choicest works of every school, a knowledge of the best that is played and sung in the world—to parody Matthew Arnold's definition of culture,—and an acquaintance with his art not confined to his own particular branch, but

[1] I hope that I shall not be understood as arguing that the *less* vocal ability a man has the better is he fitted for teaching. In arts which are learnt only by imitation the instructor must of course be, to a great extent, a model. But apart from the fact that geniuses in their own right are seldom safe exemplars for less gifted mortals, and that their very superiority would be likely to overwhelm and dishearten their disciples, there would often seem to be a real incompatibility between practical excellence and theoretical knowledge, or the power of communicating it. This arises from the radical difference between the synthetic or constructive and the analytic or critical type of mind. Thus learned grammarians are as a rule inelegant writers, and profound physiologists are not seldom indifferent doctors. Poets are by no means the best judges of verse, whilst the Pegasus of critics is too often of the Rosinante breed.

extending over the whole domain of music and reaching to its deepest principles. He must have the infinite capacity for taking trouble, which has been said to be the backbone of genius, and must spare no pains to acquire an exact knowledge of his pupil's powers, so that he may develop the good points and eradicate the bad. Whilst keen in detecting defects and strict in correcting them, he must take care not to do so in a harsh or irritating manner. This word of caution is, I am sorry to say, not altogether superfluous, for there are still teachers who, as Quintilian says, *sic objurgant quais oderint.*[1] I have myself more than once had occasion to see the evil effects on sensitive natures of such rough schooling. Patients have been brought to me who have lost all control over the voice, not from any disease or organic defect, but solely from nervous disturbance, caused by a blustering or unsympathetic master.[2] It is as though one were violently to shake and pull about a watch whenever there is the least failure in the precision of its action. The nervous system, especially in women, is infinitely more sensitive than the most delicate piece of machinery and rough handling simply defeats its own purpose,

[1] *Inst. Orator.*, lib. ii. cap. ii.

[2] Fuller's remarks concerning the *flagellant* pedagogues of his day seem especially appropriate here. He says:—"Such an Orbilius mars more scholars than he makes. Their tyranny hath caused many tongues to stammer which spake plain by nature, and whose stuttering at first was nothing else but fears quavering on their speech at their master's presence."

The true function of the educator is to foster budding talent, not to crush it.

As if the catalogue of qualities and accomplishments just recited were not long enough, a new school has arisen of late years, which demands that an exact and profound acquaintance with the anatomy and physiology of the vocal organs gained by dissection of the dead, and laryngoscopic examination of the living body, familiarity with the mysteries of acoustics, pneumatics, and hydrostatics, together with some added tincture of metaphysical lore, shall form part of the equipment of the unhappy wight who wishes to take up the profession of a singing-master.

Such multiform erudition might reasonably enough be looked for in a candidate for Teufelsdröckh's Professorship of Things in General, but it is more a hindrance than a help to the teacher whose aim should be not to make his pupil an indifferent scientist but an artistic singer. Apollo Musagetes himself, encumbered with such a load of irrelevant learning, would sink to the level of a third-rate pedant. The old Italian masters who knew little and cared less about the *science*, but were profoundly skilled in the *art* of singing, trained their pupils' voices with a success certainly not inferior to that of our modern professors armed with their laryngoscopes, spirometers, stethometers, and other *vocicultural* implements. I shall probably not be suspected of under-valuing the laryngoscope. In the hands of the physician it has undoubtedly been the means of saving thousands of lives, but in those of the singing-master I fear it is too likely tô lead to the ruin of not a few voices. The most experienced teachers and professors of the art agree in condemning the frequent use of the laryngoscope in voice-training as not merely useless but pernicious. Signor Manuel Garcia, at once the most scientific and one of the most successful of *maestri*, has informed me that in his teaching he makes but little use of his own invention. That accomplished teacher, Madame Seiler, also has never allowed her skill with the laryngoscope to encroach on the true domain of voice-training. To my mind it is just as absurd to insist on a singer knowing the structure of his vocal organs as it would be to make painters learn the anatomy of the eye and study its internal condition with the ophthalmoscope. At best the laryngoscope can only serve to make the singer self-conscious, a fatal defect in the execution of movements which to be perfect must be almost automatic. Moreover, such examination of the throat when practised by beginners is sure to cause considerable local irritation and fatigue. Again, it is only to the experienced eye that the laryngeal mirror conveys accurate knowledge of the state of the parts. The unskilled observer is apt to mistake transient and accidental appearances for signs of threatening or actual mischief; he becomes nervous, like a man who feels his own pulse, imagines that he cannot sing, and may really fail from no other cause than his self-created fear.[1] The teaching of singing by anatomy is an absurdity worthy of Laputa. What would be thought of a dancing-master who should begin his course with an elaborate exposition of the structure of the lower limbs? What would be the fate of a pupil who had learned the art of self-defence from a professor who had perplexed him with the origins and insertions of the muscles of the arm instead of teaching him to hit straight from the shoulder? One can imagine the painful disenchantment that would overtake the youth thus eruditely trained when he had to stand up to a bruiser of the old school whose knowledge of anatomy was limited to the whereabouts of the "bread-basket." Is swimming only to be acquired after a preliminary course of instruction in the laws of fluid pressure? Is the pronunciation of a foreign tongue best learned by laborious analysis of the mode of formation of the various sounds? Even in sculpture, where a knowledge of anatomy is generally considered essential, we have the example of the Greek artists to

[1] As an instance of the kind of error into which the amateur is likely to fall I may mention that mere redness of the vocal cords is not at all a sure indication of their being unfit for work. In some of the best singers the vocal cords are never of what is called *normal* colour, *i.e.* pearly white, but always more or less red. Again, in determining the functional fitness of the cords the *manner* in which they perform their movements has to be taken into account. As this depends much more on the efficiency of the nervous apparatus than on local conditions, it would not be wise for the anatomico-physiologico-laryngoscopical vocalist to trust to his own observations

the contrary. The perfection of their statues has been the wonder of all succeeding generations, yet it is all but certain that they knew no anatomy.

The first thing which the master must do is to take the measure of his pupil's ability; as Montaigne (speaking of general education) quaintly puts it: "Il est bon qu'il le face trotter devant lui pour juger de son train." Before everything it is essential that the true quality of the voice should be once for all determined. This is the keystone of the arch, and training founded on a mistaken view as to this simply vitiates the delivery throughout the whole compass. The result is necessarily failure, possibly even ruin of the voice, unless the error be discovered and rectified in time. The master cannot, therefore, be too careful in coming to a decision on this cardinal point. It is not always, however, an easy matter to recognise the "natural order" to which a given voice belongs, especially when the physiological development is not quite complete. The laryngoscope gives no help in the matter, for there are no certain signs by which a contralto can be distinguished from a soprano organ or a tenor from a bass. The educated ear is the only safe guide. Mistakes are no doubt often made, even by experienced masters, but they are probably nearly always corrected before real mischief has been done. Both Mario and Sims Reeves were, I believe, trained as barytones for some time before the genuine character of their voices asserted itself. In the case of Faure the opposite mistake was made, and the lyric stage was nearly deprived of its finest barytone.

It would be mere presumption in me to attempt to instruct singing-masters on a matter which belongs of right to their province. Common-sense, however, tells us that the voice is best fitted for that which it can do most easily and most successfully. The range of notes on which it is *at its best* is the true index of the category to which it belongs; they correspond, as a rule, with the middle portion of its natural compass. Mere pitch is not a safe guide; a barytone voice may cover the greater part of the tenor territory on the one hand, or of the bass on the other, but in either case it will be distinguishable by comparative want of clearness and resonance in the notes which lie outside its own proper limits. The untrained singer is not to be trusted in regard to the nature of his voice, for the relative ease or difficulty with which he delivers certain tones may depend on want of practice, or on bad habit. There is a saying that no man ever sees his own face in the glass; it is still more true that no one really hears his own voice. I do not mean to say that a singer should altogether disregard his sensations, and trust his voice to his teacher's discretion as blindly as a member of the "devout female sex" yields her conscience to the keeping of her confessor. If the master persists in making the pupil sing in a way that is *felt* to be a severe strain; if every lesson is followed by distressing fatigue of the laryngeal muscles, pain in the throat, weakness or huskiness of the voice, then I say, whatever be the authority of your instructor, do not listen to him, but rather heed the warning that is given you by your overtaxed organs. The most skilful and experienced teacher may err, but Nature is never wrong, and her laws have the sanction of an unfailing Nemesis. I speak earnestly on this matter, because certain singing-masters are perhaps rather less troubled with doubts as to their own infallibility than ordinary mortals. A barytone can no more be *developed* into a tenor than a thrush can be transformed into a nightingale, and a "forcing" system of cultivation can do nothing but harm. There are *maestri* of no mean reputation who appear to take Procrustes as their model, and "crack" all voices which do not come up to their ideal standard. Their defenders meet this charge by pointing to the magnificent voices that have been "created" by the same training. Are not these rather examples of the "survival of the fittest"? Exceptionally powerful organisations are of course able to bear a discipline that would be fatal to weaker vessels.

SECTION II.

Vocal Gymnastics.

Technical training must be directed to the development of the three main factors of voice, viz. the motive-power, the vibrating element, and the resonant apparatus. The right use of each of the parts concerned in production and the most advantageous management of them in combined action—the single and battalion drill of the vocal organs—must form the groundwork of the singing-master's instructions. The more ethereal regions of artistic feeling and effect, as already said, lie altogether beyond my scope.

The motive-power is of course the air-current supplied by the lungs. Proper management of the breath is a fundamental condition of good singing, and, however beautiful the voice may be in itself, it can never be used with artistic effect if the method of respiration is faulty. The first step in any system of instruction must therefore be to teach the pupil *how* and *when* to take the air into his lungs, and how to control and direct the outflow as he empties them.[1] This is really one of the most difficult things in the whole art of singing; but it must be mastered at whatever cost, for it is a vital point. In the first place, any wrong way of breathing must be corrected. This is only likely to be the case in women in whom the proper action of the diaphragm is hindered by the pressure of tight stays. It must be borne in mind that even in persons who have seen the error of their ways, and have discarded those instruments of

1 The perfection of the art of taking breath in singing is to do so in such a manner that the act is not noticed. A story is told of Lablache watching Rubini with the closest intentness *for four minutes* without being able to see him inspire.

torture, the frame may still bear the marks of ill usage, either in permanent alteration of shape or perverted function.

Frequent short exercises in respiration should be carried out both in the erect and in the recumbent position. In standing, the body should be held upright, the head kept erect, but not thrown back; the act should be performed naturally, without flurry or violence, and at regular intervals, care being taken that the collar-bone does not rise to any perceptible extent whilst the lungs are being expanded. Those who from weakness or slovenly carriage of the body habitually stoop, or let their limbs hang with a too æsthetic limpness, will find it advantageous to commence their breathing exercises whilst lying on the back. Both inspiration and expiration should be practised. In the former the objects aimed at are · first, to fill the chest-cavity adequately with a minimum of visible effort; secondly, to take breath in singing or speaking without noticeable interruption of the phrase. In the latter, on the other hand, the lungs must be emptied thoroughly, but without straining, and the pupil must strive to gain such control over the process that he can, as it were, *mould* the issuing stream of air to any shape, and regulate its volume and force so that no part of it is allowed to escape uselessly. The breathing capacity must be increased by properly directed exercises. Walking, hill-climbing, running, fencing, swimming, dumb-bell practice, are excellent means of improving the "wind" provided they are not pushed to the point of actual fatigue.

It must be distinctly understood that these exercises are only recommended for preliminary training, or as likelv to prove serviceable when no considerable vocal effort has to be made. The *prima donna* or great actor should take little or no exercise when serious strain is going to be thrown on the vocal organ, which often needs all the nervous and muscular power that can be commanded. For persons whose system is unequal to much exertion, the want of exercise may be supplied to a certain extent, as far as the lungs are concerned, by the use of some kind of "Pneumatic machine." A very good one has been made[1] in accordance with my instructions, which I recommend to every vocalist. By means of this apparatus a person can accurately estimate the amount of air which can be inspired and expired. The use of it is also valuable by way of *drill*, as one has necessarily to go through the process in a more formal and precise manner than in ordinary breathing. By assiduous practice it is possible to increase the "vital capacity"[2] in a very marked

[1] By Mayer and Meltzer, 71, Great Portland Street. An instrument of more limited usefulness, but still of decided value in many cases, has been devised by Signor N. Carozzi, whereby one can ascertain whether he breathes symmetrically, *i.e.* whether both lungs are expanded to the same extent.

[2] The vital capacity is estimated by the greatest quantity of air which can be expelled from the lungs by a forcible expiration after the deepest possible inspiration. It is measured by an instrument called the *spirometer*, but there is so much knack

degree. Maclaren, so long the Mentor of the athletic youth of Oxford, says that the effect of walking exercise has often been shown in his own person by the gain of some inches of chest-girth in the course of a short pedestrian excursion.

It can hardly be necessary to say that the breath must be taken noiselessly. Nothing can be more distressing than the gasps which often break a flood of vocal melody like the creaking of the bellows of an organ. The air should be drawn in by the natural channel, which is the nose; the mouth being used only as a subsidiary passage, when absolutely necessary. Lamperti used to say that the vocalist should take his breath and retain it like the swimmer, and there is no doubt that those who excel in these arts adopt very similar methods as regards respiration.

The old Italian masters taught that in inspiration the anterior abdominal wall should be slightly drawn in,[1] and this method was practised for more than a hundred and fifty years; but in 1855 Mandl[2] opposed this mode of breathing on anatomical grounds, maintaining that the descent of the diaphragm is facilitated by allowing the abdominal wall to be flaccid, and to project forward in inspiration. In England the views

in using it that very fallacious results are likely to be got from it by unscientific persons.

[1] The most detailed account of the method employed by one of the best of the old Italian masters will be found in H. F. Mannstein's works.

[2] *Gazette Médicale*, 1855. See also the same writer's *Hygiène de la Voix parlée ou chantée*, 2nd edition, Paris, 1879, p. 19.

of Mandl have been advocated by Messrs. Brown and Behnke, and I was myself inclined to accept these doctrines. I felt some misgivings, however, on the subject, more especially as Gottfried Weber, one of the most acute investigators who has studied the science of singing says that it is impossible to explain why it is so, but that undoubtedly the old Italian method is the best.[1] In the early editions of this work I endeavoured to harmonise the conflicting views, but further investigation of the subject has convinced me that the old *maestri* were right, and that in the abdominal cavity there is ample room for the slight descent of the diaphragm without any protrusion of its anterior walls. I hope to publish the result of my experiments and observations before long, but in the meantime I may remark that by the old Italian method complete control is obtained at the commencement of the act of expiration, and undue escape of air, *i.e.* waste of breath, is thus prevented. In other words, by the Italian system greater effect is produced with less expenditure of force. The most casual observer must have noticed that when a great muscular effort has to be made the abdominal walls are drawn in on inspiration. The diver who is going to plunge into the water, the warrior who is about to deliver a mighty blow, instinctively draws in and fixes the abdominal walls. The Scriptural phrase of "girding up the loins" may be a figurative expression having reference to

[1] *Caecilia*, 1835, vol. xvii. p. 260.

this instinctive procedure, or may be an allusion to the use of the sash or belt so commonly employed in the East. These articles of dress of course intensify the flattening of the abdominal walls, and thus artificially assist in controlling the escape of breath.

As the result of personal observation, I may remark that the old Italian style of breathing is employed by some of the finest male singers that I know, and all these persons have a wonderful degree of control over the respiratory function.

The first point in the training of the larynx itself is to insure the production of pure tone by accurate adjustment of the vocal cords. Each note must be "held" without the slightest alteration of pitch or intensity, that is to say, with perfect steadiness and evenness. This may appear a simple enough thing, but like the goose-step of the recruit it is the foundation of vocal discipline. When perfection has been attained in this, the pupil's control of his voice must be still further increased by constant practice of what the Italians call the *messa di voce*, i.e. the holding of a note in a varying scale of intensity beginning from the softest *piano* and swelling out by degrees to the loudest *fortissimo* and then back again in the same way to *pianissimo* in one breath. This is perhaps the most essential feature of artistic voice-production, and the utmost importance was rightly attached to it by the famous old Italian teachers, who made their pupils constantly practice it, and considered the possession of the power as one of the surest marks of an accomplished singer. If, as is commonly the case, the singer employs more than one register, the matter must be carefully studied, the special peculiarities of every voice being most diligently investigated. The proper use of the registers is a point of the greatest importance in teaching. Some tenors can attain a very high pitch with the long reed (chest register), and Tamberlik, Duprez, Maas, and a few others have been able to hold the  whereas most tenors experience great fatigue of the tensor muscles of the vocal cords if they sing very high notes in the chest register; indeed, the attempt often brings on serious congestion of the windpipe. On the other hand, by using the short reed (falsetto) such singers can produce charming tones without any injury to the delicate muscular apparatus of the larynx. Many sopranos can produce two octaves and two or three notes with the long reed, and do not find it necessary to shorten the vibrating element, but a large number of mezzo-sopranos can only reach their higher notes with the head register (short reed), and contraltos also usually employ this mechanism. It is in the latter class of voice that, when the shortening of the vibrating substance of the cords begins to take place, tones of a peculiar quality are produced, to which the term middle register is sometimes applied.

The Italian masters spared no pains to "unite the

registers," dovetailing the one into the other and as it were *planing* the surface of sound till the voice was smooth and uniform throughout the entire compass, and no "break" or difference of *timbre* could be detected. In the proper management of the registers lies the whole secret of fine singing, and in nothing is the skill of the master more clearly seen than in the success with which he imparts this accomplishment to his pupils. It is on this point, too, that vocal training most requires to be controlled by the physician, not of course that a medical man should presume to dictate to the singing-master what should be done, but he may certainly advise as to what should *not* be done. All I claim for science is a right of *veto* against methods which are physically hurtful. If in the attempt to develop the voice, a register, *i.e.* a particular mode of production, is forced beyond its natural limits in a given individual, the result is likely to be serious injury to the vocal organs, in precisely the same way as when the strength of any other part of the body is overstrained. It is in order to guard against evil of this kind that I have laid such stress on the necessity of dealing with every voice according to its idiosyncrasy. If a teacher mistakes his own ideas as to the registers for ultimate facts of nature, and insists on making every larynx rigidly adapt itself to his *a priori* conceptions, he cannot fail to work much mischief. He may have some brilliant successes, but his record of failures will certainly be a heavy one. Now although the physician may be incompetent to decide how a given note is to be delivered, or a particular vocal effect produced, he alone can pronounce as to whether the vocal cords are, as a matter of fact, strained or otherwise damaged thereby. One can see with the laryngoscope the excessive congestion induced by carrying a register beyond a certain point, and the almost instant return to the normal state which occurs when the register is changed. Competent authorities affirm that the example of Duprez, the French singer so famous for his high chest-notes, had a pernicious effect on other tenors who attempted, *invitâ Minervâ*, to imitate him, and too often brought on their voices the fate of the frog which strove to swell itself to the size of the ox. Training should always begin on the middle notes, and until the *messa di voce* has been perfected on them no effort should be made to extend the compass. Most teachers train the voice upwards; from the common-sense point of view, one is disposed to say that it should be developed as fully as possible both upwards and downwards. The sort of deep growl which Garcia calls the *Strohbass* register (only to be heard in the Russian Churches and in the Great Carnivora House in the Zoological Gardens) when first attempted causes violent fits of coughing, and in the end, as a rule, utterly destroys the voice.[1]

[1] Since the appearance of the first edition of this book, the interesting troupe of Russian singers has given the London public an opportunity of hearing the *Strohbass* register. A friendly critic in the *Musical World* has taken me to task for

Together with the *messa di voce* the pupil should practise *portamento,* that is to say the *carrying* of the voice from one note to another instead of *jumping* the interval. *Portamento* is in fact the passage from one note to another in an uninterrupted glide through all the intervening tones. As *messa di voce* forms the groundwork of artistic singing, so *portamento* is its chief ornament; it is, in fact, the physical basis of *expression.*[1]

Not until the rudiments of the art have been mastered by the pupil should there ornament be studied in detail. Trills, *appoggiaturas, cadenzas,* and other embellishments are of course necessary; they

comparing the exceedingly low notes referred to with the deep tones heard in the Great Carnivora House. I beg to assure him that I intended no disrespect to the Slavonic vocalists by the comparison. There is a grand majesty in the roar of these powerful animals which is extremely impressive, and, to my ears at least, not unmusical. I must, however, adhere to my statement that the production of such tones is unnatural to the human voice and must, *as a rule,* end in destroying it. The *Strohbass* register is in short a *tour de force,* and this no doubt constitutes its chief attraction to some listeners.

"*Si le difficile est le beau,*
C'est un grand homme que Rameau:
Mais si le beau par aventure
N'était que la simple nature,
Quel petit homme que Rameau!"

[1] Although *portamento* should be constantly practised in exercising the voice, in actual singing it should be sparingly used. If employed habitually and without discrimination, it gives rise to an alternate ebb and flow of sound which is wearisome, and after a time disagreeable. This defect is called in the professional slang of vocalists, "scooping."

clothe the dry bones of song with living flesh and add colour to the bare form. Moreover, the practice of such feats of sleight-of-throat is the only way of bringing out the full power of the voice, and endowing it with all the flexibility and brilliancy of which it is capable. From the hygienic point of view I have nothing to say about such matters, which belong wholly to the province of the singing-master.

The education of the *resonators* must not be neglected, as bad management of any one of the organs which fulfil this important function will mar the effect of the voice, however beautiful in itself. With respect to the epiglottis, there is little to be said, for the part which it plays in production is not well understood, and its movements, unless in very exceptional cases, are beyond the dominion of the will. The cavities of the pharynx and mouth modify the current of sound passing through them, slightly in tone and very much in quality. The right use of these parts is, therefore, a point of fundamental importance in singing. As already said, each vowel-sound has a natural pitch of its own; the bucco-pharyngeal cavity, on the other hand, is a resonator, the pitch of which varies according to the changes which take place in its shape and dimensions. There is therefore *one* position of the parts concerned (lips, mouth, tongue, palate, and pharynx) best fitted for the delivery of a given vowel, and although owing to the interference of consonants it may not be practicable to adjust the resonator with ideal exactness in every case, the standard of purity should always be kept in view and conformed to as far as possible. By skilful management of the parts just mentioned not only may purity of tone and volume of sound be gained, but the very quality or *timbre* of the voice may be to a slight extent modified and improved. This is sometimes exemplified in the case of singers whose voice in speaking is rough or disagreeable, but becomes mellow and powerful in its natural element of song. Each vowel-sound must be assiduously practised before a glass, the space between the lips, and the shape of the mouth being particularly attended to. I do not enter into details as to the mode of uttering the different vowels; these must be left to qualified instructors. No pains should be spared by the pupil to perfect himself on this point, which lies at the root of artistic enunciation, a thing too much neglected by vocalists. Without it, song loses one of its greatest charms, and the voice of "articulately-speaking man" becomes little more expressive than sounding brass or tinkling cymbal. To a person of taste, a simple ballad sung with feeling and clearness of utterance gives more delight than the finest music rendered by a voice that sounds the notes but murders or mutilates the words which they are meant to express. English singers are perhaps the greatest offenders in this way. It is not altogether their fault or that of their teachers; the predominance of consonants and closed vowels in our language makes it ill adapted for singing. It may be hinted, however, that vocalists in general are somewhat apt to look upon the words as of very secondary importance relatively to the music, and hence do not think a good pronunciation worth taking any trouble to acquire. The childish absurdity of most operatic *libretti* may possibly have something to do with this; indeed it might seem to a philanthropic artist that the best thing to do with such drivel would be to make it unintelligible. An exception must be made in favour of the writings of Wagner and Hueffer which are of genuine poetical character, but unfortunately these works are quite out of the common order. In the case of "music married to immortal verse" the highest vocal art cannot atone for defective utterance. People are sometimes inclined to wonder that poets can be indifferent to music, as many of the best of them notoriously have been; Goethe in particular, it is said, disliked hearing his own verses sung.[1] The reason may be that they look upon music almost in the light of an enemy, as by it their "thoughts that breathe and words that burn" are too often reduced to mere "sound and fury, signifying nothing."

Defects in pronunciation, however, are very often more justly chargeable to the composer than to the singer, as, from ignorance of the laws as to the pitch of vowels, syllables are associated with notes on which they cannot be properly sounded. The singer, there-

[1] He apparently could not even appreciate the beautiful setting which Schubert had given some of his own songs.

fore, finding that he must sacrifice either the purity of the musical tone or the correctness of the vowel-sound, not unnaturally prefers to preserve the former. The only remedy for this difficulty is that music should be written with an adequate knowledge of all the phonetic peculiarities of the language in which it is meant to be sung.

I may add also that composers might with advantage make themselves acquainted with the capabilities of the vocal organ, as they find it necessary to do in the case of other instruments. Too little allowance is sometimes made for the limitations of the human voice, and music is written which is, no doubt, of heavenly beauty, but which only members of the angelic choir could sing without serious risk of injury. Of all the eminent composers Handel and Rossini alone seem to have shown regard for the delicate organisation of the human larynx. These two men, standing far as the poles asunder in everything else, agreed on this one point. Before composing an opera, Rossini used to make a careful study of the vocal capacity of every member of the company which was to sing in it.[1] Even Handel, however, does not seem to have understood that the living organ is not to be depended on at all times and seasons like a mechanical apparatus. Mr. Haweis tells us that on one occasion Handel rushed into the house of one of his company, and shaking the music in the face of the

[1] Sarah Tytler, *Musical Composers and their Works*, London 1883, p. 268.

trembling artist exclaimed, "You tog, don't I know better as yourself vat you can sing? If you vill not sing all de song vat I give you I vill not pay you ein stiver!" Another time, when a *prima donna* was doubtful as to her capacity, the excited composer seized her by the arm, "shook her like a rat," and threatened to throw her out of the window.[1] Beethoven[2] in his choral works treats the human voice exactly as if it were a machine capable of going on singing for an indefinite length of time without fatigue.[3]

[1] *Music and Morals*, third edition, London, 1873, p. 171.

[2] See N. D'Anvers, *History of Art*, London, 1874.

[3] It is a mistake to suppose that Wagner's style, *quâ* style is more injurious to the voice than that of other masters. No doubt the leading parts in Wagner's operas, from *Rienzi* to *Die Götterdämmerung*, are designed on a very large scale, and are therefore trying to the voice, but this is equally true of Meyerbeer's *Prophète* and *Huguenots*, of Verdi's *Trovatore*, and indeed of any other great opera of modern times. To say that Wagner's method of treating the voice as part of the general design, or that his demand for great declamatory emphasis, destroys the vocal organ, seems to me absolute nonsense. It is true, however, that Wagner understands certain voices better than others. Thus, whilst all his soprano and tenor music is eminently vocal, his writing for the contralto and mezzo soprano, on the other hand, sometimes exceeds the limits of possibility. Such a part as Ortrud in *Lohengrin* cannot be sung properly by any artist that I have ever heard or heard of. It is another fallacy to say that Wagner drowns the voices by the orchestra. This error has arisen from the fact that most conductors let the orchestra play much more loudly than the composer intended. Wagner's own intention is sufficiently shown by the structure of his theatre at Bayreuth. This is essentially on the lines of the antique theatre, the seats rising in the form of an amphitheatre, as in the Koilon, and the orchestra being divided from the pit by a

Perfect control must be obtained over the tongue and the soft palate, and the uvula must be carefully trained so that it may always be kept at a high level, and thus out of the way of the stream of sound flowing out from the larnyx. In the high notes, and especially in the falsetto tones, the proper position of the uvula is of the first importance (see Frontispiece), and so great an authority as Madame Lind-Gold schmidt considers that purity of tone depends largely on accurate training of the uvula. This gifted lady, who unites the highest executive powers with rare didactic skill in her art, when instructing a new pupil devotes much of her attention at first to the educa tion of the uvula. In this there can be no doubt that she is right, for that little organ can not only by an inappropriate position spoil an otherwise fine voice, but by its valve-like action with respect to the nasal

solid wall sunk several feet below the level of the first row of the spectators' seats. The brass portion of the orchestra, which is actually under the stage, produces an effect which if anything is too soft. The disagreeable effects occasionally heard in the concert room never occur in Wagner's own theatre, whilst the voices rise above the orchestra, so that not only every note but every word is distinctly audible.

The absurd complaints raised against Wagner by some vocalists remind one of the story that Schnorr von Carolsfeld was killed by his performance in *Tristam und Isolde*, the fact being that the poor man died from typhoid fever! In proof that singing Wagner's music does not injure the voice I may mention that Niemann who sang Tannhäuser in Paris in 1861 is still delighting the American public; Vogl has also been singing for many years, and his voice is as sweet as ever, whilst the vocal efforts of Fräulein Matten retain the full force and purity of her early performances.

passage, it has a positive function of the highest importance. So-called "throaty" tones are often due to the back of the tongue being allowed to remain at too high a level in the mouth. This fault must be carefully avoided, and great pains must be taken that the cavity of the mouth be adjusted to the shape required for the different notes (see p. 79) without distortion of the features. Special systems of *drill* in these movements are enjoined by teachers, and provided they are intelligently applied, *i.e.* with variations in detail according to difference of physical conformation or other individual peculiarities, it does not matter much which is adopted. When the individual parts have been brought thoroughly under control, they must next be trained to act in concert. The regulation of the force of the blast which strikes against the vocal cords, the placing of these in the most favourable position for the effect which it is desired to produce, and the direction of the vibrating column of air which issues from the larynx are the three elements of artistic production. These movements must be thoroughly co-ordinated,[1] that is

[1] Physiologists apply the term *co-ordination* to the action of the controlling principle in the brain whereby the different parts of the body are made to work harmoniously together. The keeping of the two eyes parallel to each other, the act of walking, in which, whilst the two legs carry the body onwards, the muscles of the trunk keep it in equilibrium as it moves, and the eyes guide the steps, are familiar instances of co-ordinated action. In cases of disease or injury of the brain the governing power is often destroyed or suspended, and disordered movements result. Thus a patient suffering from *Locomotor Ataxy* may be seen vainly struggling

to say made virtually *one* act, which the pupil must strive by constant practice to make as far as possible automatic.

As regards the blast, the great object to be aimed at is that no air shall be wasted or expended unproductively. Just the amount required for the particular effect in view must be used. Too strong a current tends to raise the pitch, a result which can only be prevented by extra tension of the vocal cords, which of course entails unnecessary strain. Or the air may be sent up with such velocity that some of it "leaks" through before the glottis has time to intercept it, or with such violence as to force the lips of the chink a little too far apart. In either case so much motive power is thrown away, and besides, the brilliancy and fulness of the tone are lost. The *coup de glotte*, or exact correspondence between the arrival of the air at the larynx and the adjustment

to place his feet where his eyes tell him they should be put. In St. Vitus's Dance the muscles generally, or those of one part of the body, lose the power of combining for a definite end, and go through violent but purposeless movements. The double vision staggering gait and indistinct utterance of a drunken man exemplify the temporary loss of co-ordinating power. The curious feeling that sometimes comes over us of having been in precisely the same circumstances at some former time has been supposed to be due to passing loss of co-ordination of the two halves of the brain, one hemisphere lagging behind the other for a moment, and *repeating* the state of consciousness, instead of helping to complete it. The "most admired disorder" that would be produced in a choir, if each performer were to sing and play in his own time and key, regardless of the rest, is an example of want of *co-ordination* that will be intelligible to every one.

of the cords to receive it is a point that cannot be too strongly insisted on. Neither books nor dissection can teach this; the sole guide is the *muscular sense*,[1] helped and enlightened by a competent instructor.

Madame Seiler strongly condemns the system of training the voice at its maximum of intensity, the lungs being inflated to their utmost capacity, and the accumulated breath discharged at the glottis as from the mouth of a cannon. She on the contrary maintains that by practice in singing at slight breath-pressure, or *piano*, and aiming at purity and sweetness, rather than mere loudness, of tone, more complete control of the organs is acquired, and much less risk of physical injury is incurred.[2] At the same time in order to acquire the maximum power, physiology teaches us that the muscles must be regularly exercised for a short time at their full tension. According to tradition this was the invariable method of the Italian *maestri*, so that it would appear that science, if not directly useful in teaching, has at least the merit of explaining what art had already discovered. The breathing should be so much under control, and so entirely transformed as it were into sound, that the flame of a candle at a distance of a few inches from the performer's mouth should not flicker as he sings. The power of so exactly regulating the emission of

[1] This is the feeling by which our consciousness is made aware of the movements and position of our limbs. It is different from the sense of *touch*, which resides in the skin.

[2] *The Voice in Singing*, new edition, Philadelphia, 1881, p. 113 *et seq.*

the breath is a good test of whether the voice is being properly used or not. It is a point very strongly insisted on by Garcia,[1] if not originally propounded by him.

The direction of the column of sound through the mouth is another matter needing attention. It must be projected against the roof of the cavity behind the upper front teeth, from which it rebounds sharply and *cleanly* to the outside. In saying this I do not mean to rival those *maestri* who gravely tell their pupils to squirt their voices as it were out of a syringe at the back of the head, the root of the nose, and even downwards into the abdomen. Singers are conscious, however, of being able to a certain extent to direct the air-column, and this faculty can be improved by practice. When the art of breathing properly has been thoroughly acquired, it ought to become entirely *automatic.* I have seen many amateurs who in their conscientious endeavours to attend to the precepts of their instructors as to the method of breathing, have entirely lost sight of the ultimate object of singing, and in place of the perfect expression of the emotions by vocal utterance, have shown either nervous hesitation or mechanical monotony.

There must be as little action as possible of any muscles but such as directly assist the production of voice. The hideous muscular contortions of the face

[1] *Traité complet de l'Art du Chant*, Paris, 1878, p. 13. The idea is much older than the date here given, and may no doubt be found in earlier editions.

and neck, and the swelling of the veins in those parts sometimes seen in singing are the result of bad habit, or prove that the natural powers are being overstrained. Perfect art is shown in the ease and grace and absence of unnecessary or irrelevant effort with which a thing is done. The unpractised billiard player holds his cue with a convulsive grip as though he were afraid of losing it, the unskilful violinist scrapes the strings as if he were scrubbing them with a shoe-brush. A feeling of *tightness* in the throat in singing is an almost certain sign of inartistic production; it is especially felt when the voice is being used in a wrong register. The sensation is probably due to excessive contraction or even slight cramp of the muscles which form the wall of the pharynx. This "tightening of the neck" may also exist as a vice of production throughout the entire compass of the voice. It spoils purity of tone and even, to a slight extent, accuracy of pitch by altering the shape of the resonator. Constant practice on the middle notes and in *piano* singing, swelling the voice out by degrees, and instantly stopping when the tightness begins to be felt, are the best ways of overcoming the defect.

It cannot be too strongly insisted on, not less from the hygienic than the æsthetic point of view, that training of the singing voice can hardly be too comprehensive or too persevering. The grand secret of the old Italian method which is so much spoken of seems to have been simply the happy combination of common sense on the part of the master with inexhaustible patience and docility on the part of the pupil. Voices were made then for *use*, not like Peter Pindar's razors merely "to sell." Caffarelli, as is well known, was kept by his master Porpora for six years [1] to the practice of exercises which covered only one sheet of music paper. When at the end of that time the disciple meekly asked to be allowed to attempt an air, his master replied, "*Figlio mio, tu sei il primo musico del mondo.*" [2] Rubini had to serve an apprenticeship of seven years before he was considered fit to sing in public. The great lack of good voices now generally complained of, and attributed to all sorts of causes,[3] I take to be principally if not solely due to the feverish hurry and impatience

[1] George Sand, in *Consuelo* (which, though a romance, is to a great extent historical and founded on careful literary research), gives the period as eight years. She also asserts that the great singer was always known as *Caffariello* everywhere except in France.

[2] There has been a good deal of futile controversy as to whether this anecdote is to be accepted in a natural or in a non-natural sense, *i.e.* whether Porpora could actually have put the whole secret of his teaching into so small a space, or whether he intended thereby to rebuke the overweening conceit of his pupil. But surely all that a singing-master can teach is the mere *technique* of the art, and the greater part of this can be expressed by symbols which, taking up little room, can be made to mean a great deal when interpreted by a man of genius.

[3] By Rossini to the extinction of the class of singers known as *soprani* or male trebles; by Madame Seiler to the gradual rise of pitch which has taken place during the last hundred years; by Behnke to the disregard of modern composers for the natural powers of the human voice; by many worthy persons, doubtless, to the general degeneracy of mankind.

of modern life which makes pupils and teachers alike more anxious for immediate success, however ephemeral, than for lasting results. The same characteristic is seen in every branch of human activity. Crude theories supported by a handful of imperfectly observed facts are offered as scientific discoveries; literature is, for most people, represented rather by the quickly scribbled and more quickly forgotten article in the daily paper than by works matured in accordance with the Horatian precept. In an age in which shoddy-making and jerry-building lead to fame and fortune, when ingenious "professors" undertake to make the "tender juvenal" bearded like the pard in six weeks, when a memory like that of Hortensius can be acquired in a dozen lessons, it is no wonder that a few months' training is thought sufficient for the voice. Hence the unsatisfactory career of so many singers, the doubtful success, the early breakdown. The same causes led to precisely the same results even in the palmy days of Italian teaching. Does not Tosi speak with the gloomiest foreboding of the shipwreck that is sure to overtake the bark which with too presumptuous confidence braves the storm-tossed ocean of an artistic career? I would propose as a motto for musical aspirants Goethe's words *Ohne Hast aber ohne Rast.* The longer their period of training, the longer and the more successful will be their career. On the other hand, nothing can be more certain than that the consequence of want of sufficient preparation must be *failure.*

One or two points have still to be touched upon. Madame Seiler lays great stress on the importance of female voices being trained by women, and male by men. As the art is to so large an extent imitative, there may be some truth in this view. According to her, F. Wieck always instructed women with the help of trained female voices. The suggestion may seem puerile to those who teach solely by the light of the laryngoscopic lamp, and who, like the fencing-master in the comedy, think more of the *way* in which a thing is done than of the result, but if the teacher uses his own voice as an example, it seems just as likely that a woman trained entirely by a male teacher will sing like a man, *i.e.* with predominance of the chest register, as that if taught writing by a man she will write like one.

SECTION III.

Vocal Training of Children.

Teaching to be really profitable, artistically speaking, must, as has been said, be individual, that is to say it must be based on a careful study of the qualities of each particular voice. Training *en masse* is like the physicking which Mrs. Squeers was wont to administer so impartially to her unfortunate charges. Some of the voices are sure to be strained by having to sing beyond their compass, whilst the tendency (innate in crowds, especially in English crowds) which each person has to outdo his neighbour, leads them to scream and bawl in rivalry of each other. It becomes a shouting contest, in which the battle is to the strong. This is the case even in cathedral choirs, where the attempt to train is seriously made, and where the teachers are at any rate musicians. Yet it is so much a matter of common observation that choristers seldom develop into really good singers, that the mere fact of having been trained in a choir is against a young artist. The first thought of experts is apt to be "Can any good come out of Nazareth?" Of the many thousands now living who have been trained in cathedral choirs during the last forty or fifty years, the names of Sims Reeves, Edward Lloyd, and Joseph Maas[1] are alone conspicuous in the musical firmament. They are in the strictest sense brilliant exceptions which prove the dismal rule.

If cathedral training is so barren of artistic singers, *a fortiori*, still less result can be looked for from institutions without the same advantages. The instruction in singing given at Board Schools and other scholastic institutions, whether the common notation or the Tonic Sol Fa system is employed,

[1] This illustrious trio of tenors is now, alas! reduced to a duet, the youngest of them, poor Maas, the Marcellus of English song, having been cut off in the flower of his artistic life as the first edition of this book was passing through the press.

though no doubt useful for teaching the elements of music, is quite insufficient for vocal culture of a high order, as the teachers for the most part have no special knowledge or skill.

There is much difference of opinion as to the age at which systematic vocal training should commence. The weight of authority is in favour of deferring it till after puberty, especially in girls. Indeed many teachers refuse pupils before that period of life. The reasons given are that training at an earlier age would be likely to damage the voice by straining it whilst still unformed, and the general health by subjecting the system to fatigue beyond its powers. To place the question in a proper light, it is necessary to be clear as to what is meant by "training." To put a young child through the vocal athletics which the adult is rightly made to practise, would be as ridiculous as setting him to defend a wicket from the "demon bowler," or to row in the University Boat-race. But I can see no objection to his being subjected to a *certain amount* of vocal discipline as early as the age of five or six or even younger. Of course in this as in other matters the question *quid valeant humeri quid ferre recusent* must never be lost sight of. Only simple little airs of limited compass[1] should be sung, and the co-ordination of the

[1] An excellent set of songs, especially adapted for children's voices, has been composed by Louisa Gray and published by Messrs. Wood and Co. They are warranted to contain "no love and no high notes," and may therefore be trusted not to inflame either the infant's tender heart or its delicate larynx.

laryngeal muscles with the ear (which is the *conscience* of the voice) should be thoroughly established. This can easily be done by invariably correcting every note about which there may be any suspicion of falseness. There is a better chance also of getting rid of throaty or nasal production at the very outset than when these defects have become ingrained by long habit. Moreover any physical deformity impairing the timbre of the voice can be remedied much more easily in childhood than afterwards. Again the parts are more pliant and docile in early life than later on, and if it is thought necessary on that account to begin piano or violin playing in childhood, it cannot be wrong to teach the use of the muscles which play that difficult instrument, the human larynx. The immense faculty of imitation possessed by children should be taken advantage of in teaching them to sing as well as to speak. I am gratified to find that so sound and experienced a teacher as Madame Seiler[1] agrees with me as to this, and the same view has the strong support of Mr. Bach[2] of Edinburgh, and Mr. Charles Lunn[3] of Birmingham, both of whom are teachers of very large experience. It may be added that some of the very best among living singers have been trained in quite early life. I need only mention the names of such "bright particular stars" as Alboni, Jenny Lind, Adelina

[1] *Op. cit.* p. 75.

[2] *On Musical Education and Vocal Culture*, 4th ed. Edinburgh, 1884, p. 254.

[3] *The Management of the Voice*, London, 1882.

Patti and Albani. The unique voice of Madame Patey, and the rich tones of Miss Hope-Glenn have not been injured by the regular instruction they received when mere children. Catalani and Christine Nilsson also used their voices largely, almost from the cradle.[1] Who can tell how many mute inglorious Grisis and Marios there may be who have been lost to art for want of early training!

So far from injuring the general health, the teaching of singing in childhood is likely to prove highly beneficial, especially in cases in which there is a tendency to delicacy of the lungs. By the healthful exercise of these organs in singing, the chest is expanded, the muscles of respiration are strengthened, and the lungs themselves are made firmer and more elastic. The rare occurrence of pulmonary disease among singers is well known. Of course it must be understood that the vocal exercises are to be strictly moderate both as to quality and quantity, that is to say the lessons must be very short, and at the most only the ten or twelve notes which form the average

[1] All the artistes referred to have remarkably strong and durable voices, and in none of them has there been any sign of premature decay. It is true that Madame Lind *retired from the opera* at the early age of twenty-eight, but this was altogether on the score of general health. The severe nervous headaches from which this lady has suffered nearly all her life were greatly intensified by the late hours and excitement of operatic performance. Madame Lind, however, continued to sing at concerts and oratorios, and her voice retained its fine timbre, and nearly its full compass, for nearly twenty years after she had taken her farewell of the lyric stage.

compass of a child's voice must be used. On no account must there be the least forcing or fatigue. On the whole I think there can be no doubt that vocal training in childhood, if properly carried out, is not only not hurtful to either voice or health, but on the contrary distinctly advantageous to both.

It remains to consider whether training should be continued during the period of puberty, whilst the change of voice is being accomplished. The doctrine has long been almost universally held that not only should systematic training be interrupted, but singing should be altogether forbidden at that time. The popular expressions, "cracking" or "breaking" of the voice, imply that the process of change is usually of a more or less violent kind. All boys are supposed to be hoarse, to "croak" or to "lose their voice," and they are cautioned not to attempt singing of any kind for some weeks or even months. Yet it is certainly not the fact that during the transition the voice is in all or even most cases, harsh and disagreeable. I have notes of more than 500 cases of choir-boys between the ages of fourteen and eighteen, whom I examined with the special view of determining this point, and I find that in only 17 per cent. was the voice really "cracked." The common notion is probably founded on the circumstance that the condition, when it does exist, forces itself on the attention with unpleasant emphasis, whilst the absence of it naturally is not noticed. When the hoarseness is very marked, it is in all probability due not so much to the physiological process itself as to the shouting and screaming in which boys find so much delight, or to *over use* of the organs in singing, or to accidental cold, &c. I pointed out some years ago[1] that in all cases in which the voice is "broken," the vocal cords are seen with the laryngoscope to be much congested. They are often, however, somewhat red even when there is no particular harshness in the voice. The change sometimes takes place with startling suddenness, as in the case of Lablache, who is said to have passed from alto to deep bass in a single day, but it is generally a gradual process which may take years to complete itself. Thus beginning, as a rule, about fourteen, it goes on steadily till the age of eighteen or thereabouts; after that, the development still continues, though much less perceptibly, and the voice is not usually full-grown, so to speak, before twenty-eight or thirty. This protracted period of development is characteristic of the male voice, and is most noticeable in the tenor variety.

If due care be exercised there is no reason why the voice should not be used in singing during the transition period. If a boy is found to have become slightly hoarse or uncertain in one or two upper notes he must not be allowed to attempt them. In fact, he should be restricted to his middle notes, so as to avoid straining at the upper end of the scale, and give the organs time to mature themselves for the utterance of the newly-acquired

[1] Reynolds's *System of Medicine*, vol. iii. p. 430, London, 1871.

graver tones. For it will generally be observed that as the boy loses a high note he gains a low one, and these notes must be carefully but regularly trained. I have met with some exceptionally fine male voices which had been trained all through the period of change, and they have proved remarkably lasting in character, showing no signs of wear even at the grand climacteric. As an instance of this I may refer to Mr. Charles Lunn, the well known *maestro* of Birmingham, who says of himself, "My voice never broke, but went steadily down and I never stopped singing, and I have my voice now" (*The Voice*, Sept., 1886, p. 144). Every one who has had the privilege of hearing Mr. Lunn sing must have been struck by the rare union of power and sweetness in his noble voice.

The reason alleged for the ordinary practice of interdicting singing during the "break" is that exercise of parts undergoing such considerable change is likely to injure them or interfere with their proper development. It may be granted that too violent or prolonged use will do so, but reason and analogy are alike opposed to the presumption that strictly moderate exercise will have such an effect. The growth of the long bones of the limbs is at least as complex a process as the development of the larynx. It is admitted that serious damage may be done to these parts by over use of them in early life; does it therefore follow that they are to be kept altogether at rest until adolescence is complete? If this were so, instead of encouraging boys to develop their strength in running, leaping, playing football and cricket, their muscular instincts should be sternly repressed, their limbs should be kept in perfect repose, and their exercise should be taken in a perambulator or Bath-chair! We know that such a course would lead to decay rather than healthy growth, and it is difficult to see how disuse of the voice under similar circumstances can fail to induce a like result. Unless, therefore, the larynx is extremely congested and the voice utterly disorganised at the period of change, I am strongly of opinion that vocal training should be continued—of course *under competent supervision and with due precautions against overwork.*

CHAPTER V.

THE CARE OF THE FORMED VOICE.

HOWEVER well trained a voice may be, much care is needed to keep it in thorough order. There are exceptions to every rule, and there have been wonderfully gifted singers who have preserved their vocal powers almost unimpaired under conditions which might have been expected utterly to destroy them. Such privileged organisations, however, cannot safely be taken as models by others of more common mould. The fate of the earthenware pot in the fable should be a warning to those who think they can with impunity keep pace with genius. In the first place, constant practice is as necessary for the vocalist's laryngeal muscles as for the violinist's fingers, if they are to be kept supple and thoroughly disciplined to his will; the exercises should be short but frequent, and *Nulla dies sine cantu* must be his motto. Such brief snatches of "drill" are particularly necessary in preparing for a great vocal effort. It is the practice of some great singers to keep themselves in voice by frequent humming and occasional practice of trills and flourishes *à gorge déployée* during the day before a performance that is likely to make an exceptional demand on their powers. Now humming (which, it need hardly be pointed out, is phonation with the mouth closed) exercises the laryngeal muscles, whilst the bursts of "full-throated" song keep all the parts supple and obedient to the will. Of course, however, no considerable *amount* of vocal practice is advisable when later in the same day the artist's powers have to be exhibited in public.

It need hardly be said that the voice must not be abused either by being forced beyond its natural compass or by excessive violence of production. If the strings of a fiddle are screwed up too tight they will snap, and severe physical injury to the vocal organs may be the consequence of straining the voice beyond the limits of its capacity. Loss of elasticity of the vocal cords from over-stretching, rupture of some of the muscular or ligamentous fibres, or even of a blood-vessel in the throat,[1] paralysis of one or more of the laryngeal muscles, are some of the ways in which nature occasionally avenges too rough handling of her delicate machinery. Bursting of the wind-pipe, with consequent formation of a swelling in the neck, has sometimes resulted from

[1] I have lately seen in a medical paper an account of such an accident during singing (*New York Medical Record*, p. 317, March 21st, 1885).

prolonged shouting in the case of drill-sergeants and howling dervishes.

Certain modes of singing, which are right enough, artistically speaking, in their proper place, are yet in themselves very trying to the voice. I refer more particularly to what are called *staccato*[1] and *tremolo.* The former, if much or frequently practised, would in time spoil the finest voice; the short jerky snaps require such a rapid succession of delicate muscular adjustments, suddenly interrupted and repeated, that exhaustion is sure to follow. It may be compared to reading in the train, which oculists unanimously condemn for the strain that is thereby put upon the muscles of accommodation owing to the constantly changing focal distance. *Tremolo* is injurious in another way, as tending to beget a depraved habit of singing. The voice, like the hands, may tremble from emotion, and art should of course imitate this as well as other natural effects, but continual quavering is as disagreeable as the tremulous fingers of the drunkard.

A point of prime importance in the preservation of the voice is never to sing when it is felt that the vocal apparatus is not in its highest condition of efficiency. From whatever cause this may arise, whether from "cold," indigestion, fatigue, or

[1] In some few instances *staccato* singing seems to be a natural gift, no training being necessary to acquire the art. In such cases the artistic use of this striking and effective method does not seem to be attended with any injurious results.

merely the subjective sensation of not being "in voice," the singer should on no account attempt any public effort. By attention to this golden rule one of the greatest of living artists has at some cost of personal popularity kept his splendid voice unimpaired at an age when most tenors have ceased to warble. The voice should never be used in buildings of bad acoustic construction; singing in the open air, however idyllic and poetical it may be in more favoured climes, should not be indulged in under our muggy English sky. The singer who lives for his art will of course not vex his precious instrument by such outrages as screaming or bawling. His voice must never rise to the discordant key of angry passion, and even domestic squabbles must be carried on—on his side at least—

"In liquid lines mellifluously bland."

Finally, ladies of an impressionable nature must be warned that violent or prolonged weeping is likely to dull the voice as much as it dims the eyesight.

CHAPTER VI.

SPECIAL HYGIENE FOR SINGERS.

As already said, singers are athletes as well as artists, and as much or more self-sacrifice is required on their part to fit them for their arduous exertions, as for an oarsman or a runner to keep himself in form. In fact, a vocal artist must *always* be in training, and his life is therefore one of almost monastic asceticism in some ways. I have already described the course he must pursue to maintain his *voice* at its best ; it now remains to indicate briefly what he must do, and especially what he must *not* do, if he wishes to keep *himself* in good order as far as the body is concerned. It has already been stated that this has a direct bearing on the condition of the voice. Whatever therefore is good for the singer's general health is *pro tanto* beneficial to his voice. A friend of mine whose beautiful voice is well-known in London society tells me that it distinctly gained in clearness and flexibility whilst he was under severe training for the University Boat-race. Temperance of every kind is more necessary for the singer than for almost any other profession.

Alcohol, except in strict moderation, is in nearly every form noxious to him, not less from its systemic than its local effects. Though it may doubtless give a stimulus which may carry the artist successfully through a trying effort, the inevitable reaction must follow, and too often requires a further dose to counteract it. What the result of this will be after a time it is easy to foresee. I do not speak of drunkenness but of the cumulative effect on the nervous system, of the progressive drain on its powers involved in such a repeated ebb and flow of vital energy. "It must follow as the night the day" that want of steadiness, *i.e.* want of adequate co-ordinative power over the laryngeal muscles, slight at first but gradually increasing, will ensue. Most of us are familiar with the hoarse tones of the confirmed votary of Bacchus. These are due to chronic inflammation of the lining membrane of the larynx; the originally smooth surface is roughened and thickened by the irritation of the strong fluid, the cords have less freedom of movement, and their vibrations are blurred or rather muffled by the unevenness of their contiguous edges. Locally therefore the effect of alcohol in excess on the parts over which it travels in its passage down the throat, and on those adjoining them, is simply pernicious; even in a comparatively mild form it keeps the delicate tissues in a state of congestion which makes them particularly liable to inflammation from cold or other causes. If a singer feels that he needs a stimulant of some sort he should take a small quantity of claret or burgundy, or a little spirit plentifully diluted with Apollinaris or Salutaris or plain water. Pungent condiments or violent irritants of any kind should also be eschewed ; in this category I place cayenne pepper, mustard, hot sauces, ginger, curry, and the whole tribe of fiery condiments. Even tea and coffee should be taken rather tepid than hot.

In the matter of food, every sensible person is the best counsellor for himself. As Bacon most wisely says, " A man's own observation what he finds good of, and what he finds hurt of, is the best physic to preserve health." It would be easy to frame elaborate schemes of diet in which the exact weight of meat and the precise quantity of vegetables allowable should be laid down with the accuracy of a physician's prescription, but such solemn trifling can only interest the professed valetudinarian. Let a man eat to the satisfaction of his natural appetite what his palate craves and his stomach does not kick against; an adult has, as a rule, been taught what his aliment should be by that most practical physician, experience. Let him take his meals at regular intervals, and chew his food properly,[1] and he may laugh

[1] The old precept,

> " Avecques chaque dent mâchelière
> Fais la digestion première,"

is physiologically sound, though perhaps a little tedious in practice. Mr. Gladstone, with characteristic exhaustiveness, gives, I believe, thirty-two bites to each morsel. He " smashes, shatters, and pulverises " his food as ruthlessly as if it were a hostile argument.

at the highly rarefied *menus* dictated by the framers of dietetic decalogues.

Although I do not presume to dogmatise on the subject of diet, a word or two on the physiological bearings of the question may not be out of place. As most of my readers know, food is required by the body, as fuel is by a fire, for the repair of the waste of tissue that is constantly going on. This waste is greatly increased by exercise, and accordingly the harder a man's physical work is, the more food does he need. The two chief functions of diet are the formation of flesh and the generation of heat, the former being fulfilled by the *nitrogenous*, and the latter by the *carbonaceous* element. A certain proportion of both nitrogen and carbon must therefore be from time to time introduced into the system, and it is calculated that 300 grains of the former and 4,800 grains of the latter are required to keep an adult body in a state of proper efficiency. Nitrogen is mainly supplied by animal substances, and carbon by farinaceous materials, although each category contains a certain proportion of both. In this fact lies the principal objection to vegetarianism, as, in order to obtain the necessary proportion of nitrogen from such a diet, an inconveniently large bulk of food has to be taken, and an unnecessary amount of trouble is thereby thrown upon the digestive organs. Alcohol, though not a food, has a certain power of preventing tissue-waste, and accordingly strict teetotalers require more solid food than moderate drinkers. Sir Henry Thompson[1] is no doubt right in saying "that too much flesh meat is eaten by Englishmen as a rule," and there is much force in his pleading for the greater use of fish, that "savoury esculent which the pleasant and nutritious food-giving ocean pours forth upon poor humans from her watery bosom."[2] Not only the quality of the aliment, but the cooking of it is a matter of the greatest importance to a vocalist, whom indigestion may for the time rob of his voice, or what is perhaps still worse, of his ear. Not every one, however, can guard against accidents of this kind by always travelling, as I understand Madame Patti does, with a culinary artist of proved skill. The meals should be taken two or three hours before singing. Professional vocalists have a special temptation to encounter in respect of supper, which is apt to be of a "too too solid" character, often with disastrous consequences to the night's rest.

The use of tobacco in moderation may be safely allowed, but a word of warning must be uttered against inhaling the smoke into the lungs, as is done by some who use cigarettes. The smoke cannot fail to irritate the mucous membrane of the deeper air passages, which is even more delicate than the covering of the eye. I am of opinion, moreover, that the practice of blowing the smoke of a cigar up behind the palate and out through the nose is one that should

[1] *Food and Feeding*, 3rd edition, p. 31 *et seq.* London, 1884.
[2] *Last Essays of Elia: Ellistoniana.*

not be indulged in by vocalists. For the rest, smoking, unless it be in excess (a term, be it remembered, which is entirely relative), is harmless enough in itself, though the example of Mario who, when not actually singing, always had a cigar in his mouth, is one which, to use the classic phrase of the biographers of the saints, is to be "admired rather than imitated."

The clothing of vocalists is a matter of importance, and certain authors have treated it in such loving detail, that some of their pages read like extracts from *Myra's Journal*—an edifying publication in its proper place, but hardly a scientific authority. They have even invented clothes for ladies which they describe with the professional fluency of a milliner's apprentice, and puff with all the persuasive eloquence of a bagman in the "dry goods" line. I have, of course, no pretension to vie with these gentlemen in matters of esoteric female costume, but must confine myself to the general principles of dress, which are, broadly speaking, the same for singers as for other persons who study their health. The grand secret of dress is that it should be suited to the season and the weather. It is impossible, however, with the best intentions always to dress seasonably in so capricious a climate as ours. We can only try to approach the ideal standard as closely as possible. Flannel or merino should always be worn next the skin, and the outer clothing should be warm, but not heavy. The parts especially needing protection in singers are the chest and the throat. The former can hardly be kept too warm, but the latter should not be muffled up in the day time, unless the weather is bitterly cold At night, however, and above all when coming out of a warm room or crowded theatre, the throat should be carefully wrapped up and the mouth should be kept shut. If there be marked proclivity to taking cold, or if the weather is foggy, a respirator is a useful safeguard. It must be of such a form as to cover the nose as well as the mouth. A very good respirator of this kind is sold by Messrs. Roberts and Co., New Bond Street. The frame is made of felt, hardened in a spirituous solution of shellac ; this can be moulded by heat so as exactly to fit the facial configuration of any given individual. The central portion of the frame corresponding with the openings of the nose and mouth is made of a thick layer of silicated cotton which acts as a filter for noxious and irritating particles, besides drying and warming the inspired air. In addition to its utility as a preservative against cold and damp, this respirator is an efficient safeguard against disease germs, which as a rule gain entrance through the respiratory channels. I take this opportunity of acknowledging the obligation under which I am to Dr. Henry Fisher, of Chelsea, for his valuable assistance in perfecting the little invention. I am afraid, however, that most ladies would prefer to brave all the dangers of cold air and fog rather than wear such an apparatus, and the alternative of keeping the mouth carefully shut may be equally objectionable to some of them. The dress should not be too tight over any part of the trunk or the neck, so as to hinder either the respiration or the movements of the larynx. Stiff collars of the "masher" type should never be worn by vocalists; to sing with such a thing on would be like dancing in fetters. Still worse is anything that presses tightly on the chest or on the upper part of the abdomen; the voice is robbed both of power and resonance because the lungs cannot send a sufficiently strong air blast, and the cavity of the chest has no room to vibrate. As for tight lacing, where the pressure is severe enough actually to deform bones and displace organs, and where the corset resembles a surgical apparatus for fixing the ribs, it is a species of stupidity for which hardly a parallel can be found even among the innumerable follies of civilised life. I have seen a girl, who showed evident signs of suffering from this cause, smile pityingly on seeing a Chinese lady attempt to walk—a singular example of the mote and the beam!

A well-made woman should not require stays, and where some support is needed, the corset should be made of elastic material, yielding readily to the natural movements of the trunk, and with just enough whalebone to give it firmness. Steels are an abomination which should be left to the foolish virgins whose devotion to fashion makes them willing to rival the Fakir in self-martyrdom. Rigid stays, in short, should be relegated to the museums, to be exhibited side by side with the Collar, the Boot, the Maiden, and other mediæval instruments of torture.

Amongst the external things to be most sedulously guarded against by the singer must be mentioned irritating atmospheres or vapours. I have already alluded to the danger of fog; but dust, smoke—whether from chimneys or from the "fragrant weed,"—sulphur fumes *et hoc genus omne*, are all injurious. It must be remembered that the throat is as it were the heel of the vocal Achilles; it is his vulnerable part. Sitting late in hot, stuffy rooms, where the calumet of peace makes the air thick with smoke, is especially pernicious, as the heat and irritation combined make the throat doubly sensitive to cold when the outer air has to be faced.

It may not be superfluous to say that sufficient exercise should be taken by singers; it is a thing which they are apt to neglect, partly from fear of taking cold if they go out of doors, partly from a sort of physical laziness that seems in some way a part of the artistic temperament. Violent or prolonged exercise is too fatiguing for those who have to expend considerable muscular force in another direction. As already said (p. 70), on days when great and sustained vocal efforts have to be made, absolute rest should be observed. Over-heating is in a special degree dangerous for singers by reason of the increased risk of chill. In wet or foggy weather, or when a cold east wind is blowing, a vocalist should not expose his larynx by going out of doors if he can help it; but in fine weather the outer air is a useful stimulant. Walking,[1] riding, sculling, tennis playing, can all be recommended as improving the wind and giving vigour to the muscles, but nothing of the kind should be carried to excess. Hunting is almost too violent, setting aside the temptation to shout: besides, anything involving rapid motion through the air is in some measure bad for the throat, owing to the forcible impact of cold air on the pharynx, &c., and the necessary entrance into the air-passages of irritating particles of various kinds which may be floating about in the atmosphere. Fishing is not as a rule suitable for singers, as the exposure is too great. Running, or climbing hills, though good in them selves for expanding the chest, are not advisable for the vocal artist.

Coming to more special hygiene, I would impress on all singers with the strongest emphasis the importance of at once discontinuing to use the voice when they have taken cold, or when the throat is in any way out of order. Rest of course is not always possible,

[1] Women should walk not less than *three*, and men not less than *six*, miles a day. The dread of taking cold through the feet is unfounded if people will only consent to wear boots of sufficient thickness. Ladies in particular are, from motives easy to understand, somewhat inaccessible to the teachings of sound hygiene in this respect. *A propos de bottes*, I may remind my fair readers that high heels in the middle of the sole, however *chic* or *psut* they may be, are utterly unsuited for any kind of physical exercise. It is not my business to discuss other still more serious evils to which this fashion gives rise by the displacement of important organs which it entails.

and there are many who grudge, and more who can ill afford, it, even when singing is most difficult and painful. I know well how hard even a short period of enforced idleness is to an artist in the full tide of a successful career, and how sorely even a week of unproductive repose may press on the struggling vocalist. It is, however, an economy in the long run to husband for a time the powers which are the means of livelihood, that they may not be lost altogether. *Reculer pour mieux sauter* is to progress and not to lose ground—a truism, perhaps, but none the less a principle of action which is too frequently lost sight of in the hurry and struggle of our fevered modern life. I could tell of many cases occurring in my own experience where disregard of this advice, or inability to follow it, has resulted in total extinction of the singing voice, and the consequent ruin of a brilliant career.

Physicians are often asked by singers how their throats can be "hardened," and their susceptibility to cold diminished. One of the best preservatives is the morning "tub," and no bad effects need be feared from it even in winter, as long as the skin responds with a healthy glow to the friction of the towel. But a bloodless face, chattering teeth, and *chair de poule* show that the shock of the bath has been too great. In such cases, however, much good may be derived from daily sponging of the outside of the throat in the manner described further on (see p. 198). Singers may also with advantage extend their daily *toilette* to the upper air passages. The throat should be rinsed out with water, to which a small quantity of salt, or a teaspoonful of eucalyptus or any other toilet vinegar, has been added, and the nasal channels should also be cleansed in the same way. If this were done as regularly as brushing the teeth, people would be much less liable to catarrhal troubles, and voices would be clearer and less "nasal" or "throaty."

This chapter would not be complete without some mention of various substances, liquid or solid, which are, or are reputed to be, "good for the voice." All singers and many speakers have their pet nostrum, which is credited by them with wondrous efficacy in clearing, strengthening, or softening the voice, or making it "rich," "supple," &c. Most of these things are little more than "fads" (*sit venia verbo*), but they have often a virtue of their own which it is well for the practical adviser to recognise. Great is the power of the imagination, and if a man fancies that a thing does him good, it is no doubt often really beneficial to him; so in medicine the wisest counsellors are they who adapt their measures to things as they are, not as they perhaps ought to be. The truly enlightened physician is not he who, standing apart as it were on a height of pure science, denounces everything as nonsense which cannot be accounted for on mechanical principles, or demonstrated by instruments of precision, but rather he who, dealing with "this foolish compounded clay, man," as he finds him, tries to turn the patient's weaknesses into means of help. If a man is deprived of an aid which he believes to be *necessary*, he is likely enough to fail, owing to that very cause. I may remind my readers of Scott's early observation of the magical influence of a waistcoat-button upon a schoolfellow's memory. The utility of many things which vocalists deem necessary for the well-being of their throats is of much the same kind as that button: they are things which they have become accustomed to, and an association has been created, the rude severance of which might be disastrous. Therefore, as long as I do not know a thing to be actually injurious, directly or indirectly, I recommend vocalists to take whatever they suppose to be helpful to them.

The remedies used by those who for some reason or other require artificial aid before singing or speaking may be either constitutional or local, though certain things act in both ways. Medicine in the form of a draught taken shortly before singing is sometimes of great use in helping a vocalist who is obliged to use his voice when he is physically unfit either from some slight local affection or from constitutional weakness. Whether a tonic, a stimulant, or a sedative is needed, must be left to the physician to decide. A suitable remedy, taken half an hour or so before singing, may be the means of ensuring a brilliant triumph to an artist who would otherwise have broken down from mere nervousness. It is not only beginners that suffer from this paralysing weakness; the artistic temperament is so high-strung that a very slight emotion is at times sufficient to disable the powers of execution. Cicero confessed that he never mounted the rostrum without feeling as if he were going to certain failure; many great singers and actors must have had a like experience.

An amusing list is given by Mandl[1] of the things used by many celebrated vocalists for the benefit of their voices. Champagne, claret (separately or in combination), and beer figure very prominently, as might be expected; but teetotalers will be pleased to hear that coffee, tea, milk, seltzer, and lemonade have also their adherents. Others deem apples, pears, prunes, strawberries, the "sovran'st things on earth" for the voice. We may allow that all these specifics have some good effect: at any rate if not taken in excess they are harmless. The ascription, however, of voice-giving properties to such things as cold beef, sardines, and salted cucumbers, to say nothing of hot water, can only be regarded as among the eccentricities of genius. Raw eggs, either *au naturel* or beaten up with sherry, are perhaps the most widely esteemed of all specifics for the voice. There can be no doubt that many of those things are of service, and it may be well to indicate the *rationale* of their action. This is expressed in two words, lubrication and stimulation—properties which are frequently combined in the same remedy. The former effect is produced by preparations of a so-called "emollient" or "demulcent" nature, such as glycerine, tragacanth, honey,

[1] *Hygiène de la Voix*, 2nd edition, p. 66. Paris, 1879.

jellies of various kinds, custards, white of egg, &c. These substances supply grease to the wheels, if I may be pardoned the unæsthetic metaphor; they moisten the mucous surfaces—a most important office when it is borne in mind that several of the parts concerned in the production of the voice touch each other, and must consequently work at a disadvantage and with some friction if they are dry. Sometimes when the throat looks, and when at rest, feels perfectly well, yet if any vocal effort is attempted, a most disagreeable pricking or stabbing feeling is experienced at the back of the palate and the upper part of the throat. In such cases cocaine[1] in the form of soft lozenges or pastils often gives immediate relief. Stimulants are substances which, as it were, apply the goad to parts whose energy is flagging; they are of two kinds, general and local. Of the former I have already spoken, and it need only be added that they influence the voice through the nerves which govern the laryngeal muscles. The latter operate directly on the tissues of the throat, especially on its lining membrane, inducing a brisker flow of blood, and a corresponding increase of activity in its glands which pour forth a more copious secretion. Lozenges of benzoic acid or chlorate of potash are useful in this respect, and they may be made small enough to keep in the mouth under the tongue in the act of singing without detriment to the artistic

[1] Each pastil should contain one sixth of a grain of cocaine and one may be taken every half hour for two hours.

effect. Protest has already been made against violent irritants like capsicum (cayenne pepper), which is often used with the sanction of medical advice; red gum (eucalyptus), which is also sometimes recommended, is still worse. These things no doubt have their place as therapeutic agents in certain conditions of the throat, but used as popular remedies I can only compare their effect to that of a strong acid applied instead of oil to the joints of a delicate machine.

A similar objection applies to a recent invention which is extensively advertised with testimonials from several persons whom one is surprised to see led away by such a "vain thing." The Ammoniaphone, as it is absurdly called, was suddenly presented to an astonished world as a talisman only comparable to the magic rings and lamps of Oriental fiction. By simple inhalation of a little vapour—not unlike very weak smelling-salts—not only hoarseness, huskiness, and other vocal troubles were to be promptly dispelled, but the natural voice was to be transformed, so that the harsh splutterings and cacklings of our Northern throats should become softened to the melodious cadence of Italian utterance. The voice was to be "Italianised," *voilà tout*, a process simple enough to any one who had grasped the fact that the vocal superiority of the Italians arises simply from the chemical constitution of the air which they breathe! Isolation of the active principle of the said air and its application to the voice was an obvious sequence of ideas to a professor of agricultural chemistry, who was doubtless familiar with the effect of manures on poor soils. Dr. Carter Moffat would have been honoured in Laputa as much as the brother philosopher who tried to extract sunbeams from cucumbers. The method might be indefinitely extended. Why should not the fire of Italian eyes be brought hither by some chemical Prometheus and infused into our colder orbs? Or the sunbeams be disentangled from Gretchen's ripe cornfield of yellow hair, and woven into the paler web of Lucy's flaxen curls? Or to preserve the balance of exchange, why should not the concentrated essence of the bloom of a fresh English face be successfully applied to the sallow cheek of the Spaniard? Why need we despair of finding the physical equivalent of mental endowments, and thus by an alchemy surpassing that of Lully or Roger Bacon transmute the playwright of the Callipyge Theatre into a Shakespeare, or a ploughboy into a professor of Agricultural Chemistry? Reservoirs of virtue might be established, from which liars could be supplied with veracity, the angry-minded with meekness, cowards with valour, quacks with honesty, rising young politicians with modesty. A man exposed to temptation might then send for a fresh supply of integrity, and a new set of virtues might be ordered every year.

The chemical substance that is to work all these wonders on the voice is stated to be peroxide of hydrogen with which a little ammonia and some other things are combined. The instrument is a tube containing a strip of cotton soaked with the liquid, the vapour of which is inhaled through a small mouth-piece. Divested of the miraculous element the Ammoniaphone is simply a form of "dry inhaler" charged with a volatile preparation of doubtful utility. Any real effect which it may have is of a slightly stimulant nature; of its powerful influence on the imagination, however, there can be no doubt. When it was first heard of I wrote to Dr. Moffat with the view of giving the invention a fair trial. After carefully testing it on several individuals who were not informed as to the nature of the results to be expected, I can only say that in my hands at least the Ammoniaphone failed to produce any particular effect.[1]

[1] The law of evolution governs the growth of ideas as well as of organisms. It was impossible that a remedy of such thaumaturgic virtue for the throat should long remain confined to so narrow a field of action. It is, therefore, not surprising that this bottled essence of the "sweet South" has already acquired the property of relieving "abstruse bronchial and pulmonary affections." It may safely be predicted that the Ammoniaphone will continue to develop new powers in various directions, till it reaches its proper position as a *Catholicon* or *Panacea.*

"O grande puissance
De l'Orviétan!"

CHAPTER VII.

THE SPEAKING VOICE.

SECTION I.

Mechanism of Speech.

QUINTILIAN'S classification of the varieties of the speaking voice can scarcely be improved upon. According to him it may be clear (*candida*) or husky (*fusca*), smooth (*levis*) or harsh (*aspera*), thin (*contracta*) or full (*plena*), stiff (*dura*) or supple (*flexilis*), ringing (*clara*) or muffled (*obtusa*). To these might be added the hollow, nasal, shrill, and "throaty" varieties. These are the chief "natural orders" of the human voice, but in all the multitude of the earth's inhabitants it is probable that no two voices could be found exactly alike. *Quot homines tot voces.* I need not repeat here what has already been said as to the difference of the speaking and the singing voice. One striking circumstance is that not only are the pitch and intensity different, but the *timbre* is often not quite similar in the same voice when used in speech and in song respectively; in some cases, indeed, the difference is so great as to be startling. When a voice we are accustomed to hear in ordinary conversation as an unmusical and disagreeable series of noises becomes transfigured in singing into a stream of liquid melody, the effect is as if a charwoman suddenly became changed into a goddess—*vera incessu patens dea*—before our eyes. The range of the speaking voice is in most people very limited; in the majority of Englishmen it hardly exceeds three or four notes in ordinary speech.[1] Of course, however, it is *possible* to speak at almost any pitch that can be sung. The tone habitually and instinctively chosen by speakers is the middle part of the vocal compass, and it is at this pitch that the voice is used with the least effort and is heard to the best advantage. The average male voice is barytone, and its middle, according to Hullah,[2] lies between F and B♭: the average female voice is about an octave above this. Exceptionally high-pitched male voices are every now and then met with which approximate almost to the female type, and lady controversialists may sometimes be heard in the streets whose depth (to say nothing of their *breadth*) of utterance might be envied by a City toastmaster. The former anomaly is probably

[1] Mr. F. Weber, the Resident Organist of the German Chapel Royal, St. James's Palace, who has recently written a very interesting article in *Longman's Magazine* (Feb. 1887) on *Melody in Speech*, says: "Sentences are spoken in a certain musical key, and are mostly begun on the fifth or dominant of the scale of the key-note, from which they descend in seconds or thirds or other intervals to the key-notes, and, maybe, down to the dominant.

[2] *Op. cit.* p. 25, footnote.

dependent in most cases on an arrest of development; in other words, the change has either not taken place or has been imperfect. In a few such cases which I have had the opportunity of examining, the larynx seemed below the normal size in all its dimensions, presenting sometimes a striking contrast to the rest of the body, which was well grown and robust. This quasi-feminine tone of the male voice is sometimes associated with an arrest of development in other organs which undergo a natural change at puberty, but it is often due to a merely local condition. The power and volume of the speaking, as of the singing, voice depend on the force with which the lungs can deliver their expiratory blast, but much more on the size and shape of the resonance chambers. *Cæteris paribus*, a man of massive frame and capacious chest should have a stronger voice than a man of light build. When a weak voice is associated with a powerful *physique* the fault is not in the lungs but in the resonance chambers. In some cases also no doubt the management of the voice is defective.

The speaking, like the singing, voice loses much of its strength and beauty in old age. "Is not your voice broken? your wind short?" says the Chief Justice in reply to Falstaff's assertion of his youthfulness. Mr. Bright at the age of fifty-five complained that his voice was not what it had been, and in nothing is Mr. Gladstone's old age more marvellous than in the amount of vocal power which he still retains.

The mechanism of speech is practically the same as

that of song as far as the larynx is concerned, though of course the action of the vocal cords is of a less complex description. There are, however, in the speaking, as in the singing voice, at least two registers, the "chest" and "falsetto" notes being distinguishable in voices of even the most limited compass. In the act of speech there are four elements: (1) the air-blast; (2) the vibration of the vocal cords; (3) the resonance of the chest and the cavities above the larynx; and (4) the articulation or modification of the sound, as emitted from the larynx, into various forms as particles of intelligible speech. The last, which in singing is of the nature of an addition, is the essential and distinctive feature of speech. The separate elements of articulate sound are of a twofold kind: first, continuous, and secondly, interruptive. The former are the vowels, of which there are five fundamental varieties universally present in human speech wherever uttered, and an indefinite number of modified forms, some of which are heard in one tongue and some in another. The interruptive elements are the consonants, most of which, as the name imports, cannot be sounded apart from vowels; they are produced by momentary stoppage of the sound-current by means of the palate, the tongue, and the teeth. We may in fact make a fanciful picture of speech to our mind's eye by comparing the stream of sound to a river flowing between banks, now near each other, now wide apart, broken up by rocks of various size and shape, trunks of trees, small islands, and whatever else breaks the smoothness of the current; the unbroken stream of varying breadth represents the vowels, the broken and twisted current the consonants. At the risk of reminding the reader of M. Jourdain's *maître de philosophie*, something must be said as to the formation of the individual letters, but this uninviting subject will be dealt with as briefly as may be consistent with clearness.

The different vowel sounds may be said to be the result of the gradual elongation of the mouth-cavity combined with alterations in the shape and size of its external orifice produced by the varying action of the lips. The following is the order of the five vowels in relation to the length of tube required for their production, beginning with the shortest; *i* (ee), *e* (pronounced like the French *é*), *a* (ah), *o*, *u* (oo). It was proved experimentally by Czermak [1] that in the utterance of these five vowel-sounds the nasal part of the air-passage is shut off from the mouth by the soft palate with the exception of the *a* (ah) sound, where the closure is not complete. In delivering these vowels the mouth acts as a resonator, the inlet of which is at the back, and the outlet at the lips, both orifices being alike variable in length and in shape. On the proper production of the vowels depends distinctness of articulation, and the final, as it is the severest, test of a speaker's training is the perfection of his rendering those five letters, *a*, *e*, *i*, *o*, *u*.

[1] *Sitzungsberichte der Wiener Akademie* (*matematisch-naturwissenschaftliche Klasse*), Band xxiv. p. 4, March, 1857.

Consonants have been variously divided by grammarians and physiologists according to the modifica tion of the air-blast in delivering them, and, again according to the supposed anatomical factor in their production. Thus we have the division into lip-letters or *labials* (*b*, *p*, *f* *m*, *v*), tooth-letters or *dentals* (*d*, *t*, *l*, *n*, *r*, *s*), and throat-letters or *gutturals* (*g*, *k*, *h*, *j*), and the more scientific, but less practically convenient, classification into *explosives*, *resonants*, *vibrants*, and *aspirates*.

Provincial and national varieties of accent probably depend on slight physical differences in the mode of producing the various sounds, which again may be, in a certain measure, due to minute ethnological differences in the conformation of the organs.

SECTION II.

Defects of Speech.

The speaking voice varies much according to the state of the bodily health and of the mental emotions. Thus without any structural disease of the larynx it may be reduced almost to a whisper by the exhaustion of a wasting illness. Want of food has a marked effect on the volume of the voice, making it thin and hollow. Anger makes the tone harsh, whilst pity or love makes even an unmusical voice "soft and low." Excess of joy, sorrow, indignation or terror, may take away the power of speech—an effect expressed by Virgil in the well-known phrase, *vox faucibus haesit.*

This is no doubt due to a momentary paralysis of the cords from the shock to the nervous system, sometimes also to drying of the natural secretion of the mouth from a similar cause.[1] To be able to imitate all these different natural effects whilst retaining full control over the voice is the highest perfection of oratory or acting.

Some account must now be given of various defects of speech, some of which arise from more or less obscure natural causes, whilst others are due to vicious habit, to carelessness or to affectation. The former category includes stammering and stuttering; whilst under the latter head I place such faults as lisping, speaking with a nasal or "throaty" twang, insufficient opening of the mouth, &c. Stammering and stuttering affect the voice at the very fountain head of its production, whilst the other defects arise from malformation or bad management of the upper resonance chambers. Again, whilst stuttering, stammering, and lisping are diseases or errors of *speech*, the others principally affect the quality of the *voice*, though they may also mar the distinctness of the utterance.

A distinction must be made between stammering and stuttering, although they are often used even by scientific men as interchangeable terms, and indeed the difference is not very easy to define. One has only to glance at the varying and sometimes contra-

[1] The sudden arrest of the salivary secretion through fear is or used to be employed for the detection of criminals in India. The ordeal was the swallowing of a handful of dry rice, which the *mens conscia recti* made easy, but the sense of guilt impossible.

dictory accounts given by writers on the voice and on elocution, whether from an artistic or a medical point of view, to become aware of the confusion in which the whole subject is involved. The inherent difficulty of the question is due to the impossibility of observing the mechanism of the defect by actual inspection; we are therefore thrown back on more or less plausible theorising. In the following brief account I will try to confine myself to *facts* as far as that is possible in a matter in which nearly everything is doubtful.

If we attentively observe several persons afflicted with an impediment in their speech and compare them one with another as regards their manner of utterance, a radical difference can hardly fail to be noticed. Leaving minor points out of consideration, it will be remarked that while one class of persons find their chief difficulty in *uttering sound* of any kind, another cannot force their *organs of articulation* [1] to do their bidding. In the former case (stammering) it is clear that the larynx is at fault, whilst in the latter (stuttering) the seat of the trouble is the "unruly member" the tongue, or the lips.

Stammering may be due to inability to control the

[1] Dr. Holger Mygind, of Copenhagen, in the excellent translation which he has made of this little book was puzzled as to how he should render the word "stuttering" there being no distinction in Danish between "stammering" and "stuttering." He has accordingly invented the terms "stammering of phonation" and "stammering of articulation" as equivalents for our words, a nomenclature which appears to me even better than that used by us.

action of the vocal cords sufficiently for phonation, or it may be the result of spasm of the diaphragm, which renders it impossible to send an air-blast up to the glottis.

Stuttering, on the other hand, arises either from spasm of the tongue, *i.e.* strong contraction of the muscles which govern its movements leading to immobilisation of the organ at the bottom of the mouth, or from imperfect control over the lips. The stammerer's efforts to sound his voice are very painful to witness, as he has the appearance of struggling for breath; the stutterer's contest with refractory letters and the "damnable iteration" of self-repeating syllables too often excites laughter rather than sympathy. In very bad cases both forms of impediment may co-exist, the sufferer being rendered almost unfit for society. It has been calculated that the proportion of the *linguâ capti* to the rest of the population is as high as one in 3,000, the great majority being males. In about 50 per cent. of a total of 200 cases Hunt[1] was able to trace the defect to a definite cause, or rather to refer its onset to a particular epoch of time. In some cases the impediment seemed to be the result of an acute illness (whooping-cough, measles, &c.), in others sudden shock to the system (fright, &c.) had been the starting-point. In a certain number the affection was distinctly of mimetic origin, that is to say, it had been produced by mimicry conscious or unconscious. In about 15 per cent. of the whole

[1] *A Treatise on Stammering and Stuttering*, Lond. 1870, p. 341.

number hereditary influence was present, and no doubt played an important part in engendering the defect. One remarkable point of difference between stammerers and stutterers is that whilst the former are, as will be readily understood, just as incapable of singing as they are of speaking properly, the latter regain control over their rebellious organs when they sing. Stuttering is made much worse by the consciousness of being observed, and, like chorea, it has the property of inducing similar attacks in persons subject to it, probably by nervous sympathy. Thus if a stutterer who may happen to be speaking fairly well should overhear a fellow-sufferer in the throes of a struggle with the common enemy, he too will in all likelihood begin to stutter. Many stutterers who have no command over their organs of articulation in ordinary conversation succeed perfectly well in formal speaking or declamation when the voice has to be produced slowly and with some effort. It must not be forgotten that stuttering occurring in a person with no previous impediment in his speech may be a symptom of disease of the brain. The effect of alcoholic intoxication on the utterance need not be dwelt upon further than to point out that the tendency is to jumble syllables and words together, and to slur all the consonants the pronunciation of which requires any complexity of muscular action. Lisping need not detain us long: it is often a mere vicious habit or stupid affectation, but in some cases where the tongue is too long for the mouth its tip is apt to get between the teeth, and thus convert what ought to be a sibilant into an aspirated dental letter (*th* into *s*). Some persons seem incapable of pronouncing *r*, the other liquid *l* being the sound most frequently substituted; the use of *w* for *r* is, as a rule, nothing more than a trick of the languid dandyism of the "better vulgar," to use a happy phrase of Warburton's, but occasionally it is due to weakness of the muscles which push the tongue forward, and the defect may be noticed in persons free from any trace of affectation. The Cockney difficulty with the aspirate is an error of breathing rather than of articulation; it is often associated with increased *intensity* of utterance, as when the speaker wishes to be emphatic. I have distinctly heard this "augmentative" *h* even from the mouths of Italian singers when a phrase had to be begun on a high note delivered *fortissimo.* The process of equitable adjustment, whereby the Cockney, whilst dropping the *h* in the right place,[1] conscientiously inserts it in the wrong, is an instance of the same spontaneous rhythm which makes the Scotchman not satisfied with making a long *o* short unless he restores the balance by lengthening a short *o* in the same phrase, or *vice versâ.*[2]

Actual *disease* of speech (technically called "aphasia," *a* priv. and *φημί* I speak), although most interesting from a scientific point of view, does not concern

[1] 'Arry had his prototype in pronunciation as well as in name in the *Arrius* ridiculed by Catullus:

"C*h*ommoda dicebat si quando commoda vellet
Dicere, et *h*insidias Arrius insidias," &c.

[2] e.g. *Brōde rŏd* for *broad road.*

us here, as the affection is not in the vocal organs but in the nervous centres which preside over them and over the faculty of language, as distinguished from articulation.

SECTION III.

Deformities and Diseases of the Organs of Speech.

The natural deformities which interfere with proper enunciation are, first, fixation of the tongue by a little fold of membrane binding its tip to the floor of the mouth ; secondly, fissure of the palate, the gap being of variable length and width ; thirdly, closure of the posterior openings of the nasal passages by membrane or bone ; fourthly, partial closure of the glottis by a membranous web between the vocal cords. The first should always be looked for in new-born babes, when it is remediable by merely nicking the retaining band or "frænum." We sometimes, however, meet with adults whose articulation might be improved by a similar operation. A person with cleft palate is at once recognisable by an experienced ear, his speech having a strong nasal twang, besides a characteristic indistinctness and want of ring. Closure of the posterior nares is very rarely found as a congenital condition, but it is evident that it must act principally on the pronunciation of the so-called "nasal" consonants ; thus *m* would become *b*, and *n* *d*, in the way familiar to most of us as a consequence of "cold in the head." A membranous web in the larynx would, it is evident, make phonation impossible.

As regards diseases affecting the voice and speech,

their name is legion. In the larynx itself there may be paralysis on one side or both of the muscles which approximate the vocal cords, or of those which stretch the cords ; this may arise either from division of the nerves supplying the muscles, just as telegraphic communication is interrupted if the wire be cut,[1] or from pressure on the nerve, if sufficiently strong to destroy its conducting power. On the other hand, the cords may be paralysed mechanically, *i.e.* their freedom of movement may be interfered with by swelling of the contiguous parts. Again, there may be actual degeneration of the laryngeal muscles themselves, as in wasting diseases. Warty growths on the vocal cords make the voice hoarse, and eventually reduce it to a whisper. Thickening of the vocal cords produces huskiness of voice. We have already seen that alcohol can bring about this state of things, but there are several other disorders, such as chronic inflammation, consumption, &c., which have a like effect. Phonation is to some extent possible even without vocal cords, and when both cords have been cut away or destroyed, vocal sounds can still sometimes be produced by the approximation of the ventricular bands and the upper margins of the larynx (ary-epiglottic folds).

[1] A well-known actress suffers from such a want of nervous supply to one of her vocal cords, the *recurrent* nerve having been severed in an operation for the removal of a small growth in her neck. The use of the voice is attended with greater fatigue than formerly, but her vocal power is still good, the sound cord doing part of the other's work by crossing beyond the middle line to meet it.

Enlargement of the tonsils gives the voice an unpleasant throaty character, which is unmistakeable after it has been once heard. The soft palate may be destroyed, or it may be unnaturally adherent to the back wall of the throat, or, lastly, it may be paralvsed (as after a severe attack of diphtheria). The effect on the voice depends in each case on the capacity or incapacity of the organ to close the upper part of the throat which leads to the nasal passages. When paralysed, its function as a valve is abolished, and it hangs as a mere foreign body in the middle of the throat, giving additional indistinctness to the utterance.

The slighter forms of disease (congestion, relaxation of the lining membrane, "clergyman's sore throat") which merely impair the clearness of the voice or render it intolerant of the least exertion, are far more common ; in fact, from the medical point of view, they make up the bulk of the vocalist's special troubles. Congestion expresses a state of things in which the blood-vessels of a part are distended to such an extent as to induce local swelling and redness; the circulation at that spot, without having actually stopped, is slower than it should be. In fact, congestion is the first step towards inflammation, and it is this which makes it, though not in itself of much importance, a condition to be got rid of as soon as possible, for it is like a smouldering fire, which a trifling breeze (*e.g.* cold or persistent irritation) may easily fan into a fierce conflagration. The nasal passages may be blocked up by bunches of small glandular growths, which hang from the vault of the pharynx like stalactites from the roof of a cave, and fill up the space between its posterior openings and the back of the throat, high up behind the soft palate. A peculiar want of resonance or "deadness" of tone is imparted to the voice by the presence of these soft masses. They are often associated with a certain degree of deafness, and the affection seems almost peculiar to cold damp climates, being particularly common in Denmark[1] and on the shores of the Baltic. In this country, however, the disease is more frequently met with in proportion to the care and skill directed to the discovery of it. Other causes of obstruction of the nose or impairment of its function as a resonator are swelling of the highly vascular tissue which covers the spongy bones (see p. 190), accumulation of dry and hardened mucous secretion, and growths within the nasal passages. Of these the ordinary soft, jelly-like polypus is by far the most common, but in certain rare cases masses of stone-like structure and consistence are found. Deformity of the partition between the nostrils, resulting usually from direct violence, such as a blow or fall, may quite alter the character of the voice.

The speech may be made "thick," or the power of articulation may be all but destroyed by swelling or ulceration of the tongue. This is usually due to serious,

[1] This disease was first recognised by Dr. Meyer, the distinguished physician of Copenhagen and described by him in 1868 (*Hospitals Tidende*).

if not dangerous, disease, the effect on the voice being a comparatively trifling part of the mischief. I have, however, seen some cases in which the act of speaking was made very trying by an irritable condition of the tongue, which made it impossible for the patient to pronounce certain letters, *e.g.* dentals, without pain. In such cases there is no actual disease, but the ailment is probably connected in some way with disorder of the digestive canal. A very similar state of things may be induced by over-indulgence in tobacco, or by the continual pricking of a broken tooth. Some of the glands under the tongue may become enlarged, or one of their ducts may be blocked up by a small piece of solid matter; in either case, the movements of the organ are greatly interfered with, and distinctness of utterance is proportionately impaired. The tongue, however, although of primary importance for articulate utterance, is not absolutely essential to speech. Persons from whom the whole of the organ has been removed can yet speak intelligibly, though, of course, with the loss of the lingual consonants. Thus the supposed miraculous occurrences, of which there are several recorded in history, of persons having their tongues cut out by persecutors and yet preserving the faculty of speech, are paralleled in the experience of many modern surgeons.

Want of the teeth, especially in front, is a well-known cause of mumbling, the *ἕρκος ὀδόντων* being an important element in distinctness of enunciation.

CHAPTER VIII.

THE TRAINING OF THE SPEAKING VOICE.

SECTION I.

Necessity of Training.

TRAINING of the speaking voice may almost be called one of the lost arts. One is filled with amazement on reading the elaborate and protracted culture which was thought necessary in ancient times for any one who wished to succeed as an orator. Of course it must not be forgotten that the art of public speaking was then a thing of far greater importance than it is in these days of cheap newspapers and free libraries. Setting aside the purely intellectual discipline, the physical education was of so minutely careful a nature that one might suppose at first sight that the pupil was being prepared for the palæstra rather than the rostrum ; indeed, no prizefighter in the good old days of the "ring" could have been more conscientiously trained. Demosthenes improved his wind by reciting verses whilst running up hill ; he declaimed on the sea-shore that he might become accustomed to the *murmura magna* of a turbulent assembly; he practised speaking with stones in his mouth with the view of making his utterance more free and distinct.[1] Cicero underwent great labour in preparing himself for public life; for several years he travelled about from place to place in order to have the advantage of the best teaching, indefatigably seeking to gain from each master whatever good was to be got from him. We can partly see the result of all this labour in reading his orations when we reflect that the man who spoke these long harangues, with an emphasis and action of which we have but little notion nowadays, was of slight physique and delicate constitution. Quintilian's precepts range over the whole moral, intellectual, and physical nature of man, and the comprehensive course of education which he considers necessary for a public speaker, apparently commenced almost in infancy. As regards the voice itself, this early discipline was probably altogether wholesome. If there is any doubt as to when it is best to begin the training of the singing voice, there can be none, I imagine, as to commencing the education of the speaking voice. It can hardly be begun too soon; in this way faults of production and articulation can be prevented, or, as it were, strangled in the cradle,

[1] Plutarch says that Demosthenes was afflicted with an impediment in his speech, and that he adopted the plan above referred to in order to acquire more complete mastery over his vocal organs.

which in after-life can only be got rid of with infinite trouble and vexation of spirit. Too much stress cannot be laid on the importance of surrounding a child even before it can speak with persons whose accent and utterance are pure and refined. The Greeks at their period of highest culture were keenly alive to the necessity of this, and would allow no servants near their children but such as spoke correctly. In England, however, the early lispings of the future orator or preacher are too often left at the mercy of ignorant nurses. We sometimes see people most particular in their choice of a French or German governess, and rejecting a better educated person who has had the misfortune to be born in Switzerland. Nay, the French teacher must be of pure Parisian growth (in spite of the fact that the best French is heard on the banks of the Loire), but it is seldom indeed that any such care is taken in the selection of the English domestics, among whom the child's early years are in great measure spent. This refers only to such matters as accent and grammatical forms of speech; it would of course be altogether Utopian to suggest that a competent instructor might with advantage be engaged to guide the little prattlers in their early attempts at voice-production. Some care might nevertheless be taken to choose nurses with musical voices and a certain amount of refinement of utterance. The fact is, however, that, as already pointed out by Hullah[1] some years ago,

[1] *Op. cit.* p. 5.

the public mind requires to be educated on this matter before it can be got to recognise the necessity of any teaching at all for the exercise of what is supposed to be a gift of nature. It is true that men speak apparently as easily as they walk, but it must not be overlooked that both walking and speaking have to be *learnt*, sometimes with considerable difficulty. Now though a boy may no doubt teach himself to walk, it by no means follows that he will teach himself to walk *gracefully*. Every one, however, will agree that very much may be done in this way by proper instruction. Again, although the human throat may "warble its native wood-notes wild" without assistance from singing-masters, it is universally allowed that the voice gains immeasurably both as regards its possessor and his hearers by skilful teaching. But it is difficult to convince many persons that the act of speaking is just as much an art that has to be acquired, and which only careful culture can bring to full perfection. I am persuaded that if there were a thoroughly qualified instructor in elocution (including in that term the whole art of voice-production apart from singing) in every school in the kingdom, our noble English tongue would lose its undeserved evil reputation for harshness of sound; much torture would be spared to the "general ear," much weariness to our auditory nerves (unnaturally strained to catch the sense drowned in a stream of half-articulate gabble), and much suffering would be saved to throats ruthlessly stretched and cramped and "every way abused" in the fierce struggle to deliver the message which the speaker has in him. It is no exaggeration to say that bad elocution is at the root of most of the throat-troubles which beset public speakers, and for that the want of proper training is almost entirely responsible. This is, in an especial degree, true of clergymen, to whom a right delivery is of more importance than to any other class of speaker. Using the voice as they do only at intervals, and then for a considerable time without pause, they are particularly liable to suffer from huskiness, difficulty of production and pain in speaking. A proper delivery would do much to avert this, and it would be well if a man's skill in the use of his voice were tested before his admission to orders. A few of the bishops, or, rather, their chaplains, I believe, do make such an examination in the case of candidates for ordination, but it is conducted in a very perfunctory manner. The Bishop of Lichfield, Dr. Maclagan, attends to this matter, I am told, with more solicitude than his brother prelates, and the result is that his diocese already shows a higher standard of elocution. In some of the theological colleges, more attention is beginning to be given to the laws of emphasis and clearness of utterance.

A very important aid to the development of the voice in young children is exercise for several hours a day in the open air. The romping is more boisterous than indoors, and the "young barbarians" have to shout and call to each other in a louder key—to the discomfort, no doubt, of neighbours afflicted with "nerves," but to the great advantage of their own vocal organs. Rousseau[1] maintains that peasant children not only have better voices than those of the well-to-do who live in towns, but that they articulate more clearly, owing to the necessity of making themselves understood at greater distances. Rabelais, who, besides his other accomplishments, was one of the most learned physicians of his time, makes the young Gargantua practise shouting every day as a healthy exercise.[2] This effect of living much out of doors is not confined to children; one may nearly always recognise a person who spends much of his time *sub dio* by the ringing tones of his voice. Miss Braddon, the distinguished novelist, tells me that she has often been struck by the fine voices heard among gamekeepers and huntsmen; and many people must have admired the melodious far-reaching cry of the Newhaven fishwives. I am inclined to attribute the vocal superiority of the Italians in some measure to this cause. Every one who has travelled in Italy must have noticed how often trades which in our climate have to be pursued indoors are there carried on in the open air. Tailors, shoemakers, tinsmiths, &c., work *al fresco*, making the streets ring the while with noisy, but not unmusical, chatter. The balmy atmo-

[1] *Émile; ou, De l'Éducation*, livre i.

[2] "Et pour s'exercer le thorax et les poumons crioit comme tous les diables."—Livre i. chap. xxiii.

sphere, as it were, coaxes the mouth to open wide, and the demonstrative nature of the people finds natural vent in loud and emphatic utterance. On the other hand, it is a common reproach to Englishmen when they attempt the pronunciation of a foreign tongue that they will not or cannot open their mouths, but make a rumbling gurgling sound in their throats, which is presently hissed or spluttered out through the set teeth, as if the speaker were afraid to open his mouth too wide for fear anything should get into it. This may be a wise precaution in a climate like ours, and Milton apparently attributes our mumbling habit of speech to this cause when he says: "For we Englishmen being farre northerly doe not open our mouthes in the cold air, wide enough to grace a southern tongue, but are observed by all other nations to speak exceeding close and inward."[1] It has also been said to be due to our reserved and undemonstrative nature which leads us to avoid making ourselves conspicuous. Whether this be part of our national character we must see ourselves as others see us to determine. At any rate, whatever be the amount of our retiring modesty that stays at home, our travelling countrymen do contrive (against their will, it may be presumed) to make themselves the observed of all observers wherever they go. And it may be asked, is the climate of Scotland more genial or the character of its people more effusive than ours? Yet Scotchmen have the gift of articulate speech,

[1] *Tract on Education*, 1644.

and display considerable aptitude for acquiring the pronunciation of foreign languages, especially of those in which open vowels predominate.

Whatever be the cause of our peculiar manner of speaking there can be no question as to the utter badness of it. Nor is there any reason why this national reproach should continue. To any one who has been fortunate enough to hear the noble tones of some of our great orators, or the elocution of some (alas! too few) of our dramatic artists, the notion that English is an inharmonious tongue may well seem absurd. The music is there, but it needs an instrument to give it voice, and the instrument again must have a player! "There's the rub!" It is not the vocal organs that are at fault in most cases, but the method of using them. This, as already said, must be taught, and to be helpful the teaching must be of the right kind. This brings me to the qualifications requisite in the instructor who undertakes to train the speaking voice. Although to some extent these must coincide with the powers and attainments already (p. 58 *et seq.*) postulated in the singing-master, the professor of elocution must have certain qualifications peculiar to himself. In the first place, it is much more necessary in this case that the teacher should himself be a good performer. Although a man may perhaps be able to teach singing without a voice, speaking can for the most part be taught only by example. Again physiological knowledge is of more incontestable advantage to a teacher of elocution than to the *maestro,* for whilst the latter has to do with parts either wholly or in great measure beyond the pupil's control, the former by knowing how the lips and the tongue should be used can not only *show* them acting properly but make the pupil imitate the movements, with his eyesight as well as his muscular sense to help him.

No man can really teach the art of utterance who is not familiar with the mechanism of articulation in all its details. Not only this, but he should know all possible defects of speech and their causes; provincial and ethnological peculiarities of accent and intonation, and the natural modes of expressing the emotions in their subtlest shades of degree, and infinite variety of kind, whether by the play of the facial muscles, or by gesture or bodily attitude. In addition to this the elocution-master should possess at least some amount of that indefinable moral force known as "personal magnetism." He should be able not only to instruct his pupils, but to command their respect and if possible rouse their enthusiasm, for, as Quintilian well says, "we more readily imitate those towards whom we are well disposed."[1] He must not be so much wrapt up in his own art as not to distinguish physical incapacity from carelessness or want of will and he should have sufficient knowledge to lead him to recognise or suspect disease or natural defect. I do not mean that he should be able to make a diagnosis,

[1] "Vix autem dici potest quanto libentius imitemur eos quibus avemus."—*Inst. Orator.* Lib. ii. cap. ii.

still less that he should attempt to treat such cases. Both these things belong strictly to the domain of the physician, and all I am asking from my ideal *phonascus* is that he shall know where his art stops and medical advice must be sought.

As wrong methods of teaching are not only useless but positively harmful, it is advisable to go at the outset to the very best instructor that can be found, otherwise the pupil may have a stock of acquired faults in addition to his own natural defects to be eradicated. Timotheus, a famous music-master of old, used to charge double fees to those who had been under other teachers before coming to him, on the ground that in such cases the labour was so much heavier than when he had no already formed evil habits to contend with. But though good teaching is absolutely necessary, the best can do little without assiduous practice on the part of the pupil. This exercise must apply to all the various sounds of articulate speech, which must be practised separately, and in combination; to the time and manner of taking breath, and the mode of using it to the best effect; to the development of the strength and compass of the voice, and to the instinctive adaptation of it in pitch and intensity to the acoustic peculiarities of whatever place one has to speak in. The registers of the speaking voice have to be "equalized" as in the singing voice, although of course not to the same degree of finish.

SECTION II.

Effects of Training.

A speaker should have his voice under control just as much as a singer, so that he may raise or lower it at will with ease and accuracy, without shrieking at one end of the scale or growling at the other. I believe that singing might with advantage be taught as an aid to elocution. The organs of the voice and those of hearing would thereby be drilled to work together, and the speaking voice would gain in volume and flexibility. In making this suggestion I would not be understood as wishing to add to the afflictions of life by letting loose on society a host of tuneless minstrels. From my present point of view I look upon singing merely as a vocal exercise, more difficult in itself, and calling the various parts of the apparatus of phonation into more vigorous play than speaking. The practice of the greater accomplishment can, I think, hardly fail to be useful towards acquiring a mastery of the lesser, and a man who has been taught to sing is on that account more likely to speak well, "as those walk easiest who have learnt to dance."

It does not follow from this that singers make the best speakers. George Sand has remarked that the singer can speak properly only in song, which is his true medium of expression. In speaking the singer is too conscious of his voice, too obviously intent on producing it according to the rules of art, to rouse the feelings, or sway the passions of his hearers, like a great orator. The singer is *vox et præterea nihil* and is therefore bound to display his gift to the best advantage; whereas to the orator the voice is no more than a vehicle, and only conveys the message he has to tell in the tones most likely to produce the effect intended. Thus a harsh voice may often be a more appropriate and effective organ of expression to an orator than the linked sweetness of a smoother utterance. As an example of this I may be allowed to refer to one of our cleverest melodramatic actors, whose ordinary tones are so melodious that one might fancy bees had sweetened his lips with honey, as they are fabled to have done to Plato in his cradle. But when the sterner emotions have to be expressed, when the stage has to be drowned with tears, or the general ear cleft with horrid speech, his accents sometimes leave the heart unstirred. At such moments ruggedness of speech and broken utterance, though inartistic and unmusical, are more expressive of human passion.

There are, however, certain defects of utterance which, though characteristic of violent emotion in some individuals, are so disagreeable in themselves that they should not be rendered too faith fully. Thus in many persons the voice becomes *throaty* in moments of excitement, that is to say, instead of being clearly delivered it is, as it were, strangled by an involuntary tightening of the internal parts of the throat. In persons of a perfervid temper, the tempest and whirlwind of passion are often accompanied by actual spasm of the throat, which literally chokes the voice. The speaker may sometimes be seen to clutch at his throat as if to pull the passage open. The tendency to *gutturalise* passion is a great drawback, and mars the effect of the finest art. One of the most accomplished of our actors, who in modern comedy is unsurpassed, has this defect to a certain extent in serious drama. Again a naturally poor voice may be managed with such consummate art that its very defects are unperceived, or in some cases become beauties to the ear of the fervent admirer. A conspicuous instance of this may be observed in the charming and accomplished lady, who is one of the chief ornaments of the English stage at the present day. Her voice, which Quintilian would have called "*fusca*," is used with such admirable skill, and is so *informed* (to speak scholastically) by the quality of her richly endowed and sympathetic nature, that more purely musical accents sound flat and uninspiring after hers. Many voices otherwise of no extraordinary excellence of *timbre* become thrilling with pathetic beauty in moments of deep emotion, when the voice seems as it were to quiver through a well of tears. On the other hand the want of this sympathetic ring in a voice naturally melodious and carefully trained has prevented a living actor from attaining the full success which his classic purity of enunciation, perfect elocution, intellectual culture, and refined method, would otherwise entitle him to. A *cold* voice, however noble, is like a beautiful face without expression. The worst of it is that the defect is one which neither study nor labour can remedy.

All other shortcomings may be amended, and even those to whom nature has been most stepmotherly in respect of vocal endowment need not despair. De Quincey says somewhere, that a mean personal appearance is often an advantage to a man by the additional incentive which it gives him for striving after real distinction. In the same way an aspirant to oratorical or dramatic honours may find a naturally poor voice a help rather than a drawback in the end. The greatest English actor of the present day has shown how much may be done by perseverance to develop the powers of an organ naturally wanting in flexibility. By a *labor improbus* worthy of Demosthenes, his voice, which in ordinary conversation is weak and rather monotonous, has been so perfected that on the stage it is rich and sonorous and can be harsh and strident or exquisitely tender at the will of the speaker. Only in moments of the most intense tragic passion is any inadequacy of the instrument perceptible, and even this is considered rather a beauty than a blemish by thoroughgoing admirers.

The advantage of training is also seen in the case of many of our pulpit orators. In Mr. Spurgeon's case the configuration of the front teeth and lips is unfavourable to effective utterance, but the vocal instrument is so perfect and the artistic expression so faultless, that neither advancing years nor ill-health can destroy the sympathetic quality of his rich voice. Such a speaker is a natural orator who unconsciously and without effort acts in obedience to laws to which those less gifted learn to adapt themselves only by a process of laborious training. The vocal powers of but few clergymen are equal to those of Mr. Spurgeon, the Bishop of Sydney (Dr. Barry) being perhaps his closest rival. Cardinal Manning and Mr. Haweis, though so different in their styles, both show how much may be done by the intelligent culture of a naturally weak organ. The former preacher makes up by extreme clearness of articulation for the lack of power in his voice, whilst the latter accomplishes the desired end by the variation and contrast of his tones, a method which, on the other hand, is perhaps carried to some excess by Dr. Parker. The sudden transitions from a deep bass tone to notes of almost falsetto quality, which characterize the style at the City Temple, would have long since caused serious injury to the larynx had not the organ itself been very strong and capable of the greatest endurance.

SECTION III.

Details of Training.

The *principles* on which the education of the speaking voice must be conducted have already been sufficiently explained; they may, however, be recapitulated in the following propositions:

1. Training must be begun almost as soon as the child can speak.

2. The voice must be strengthened by frequent exercise, not only indoors but in the open air.

3. Whatever be the natural endowments of an individual, proper teaching is necessary

4. Singing is a help to good speaking, as the greater includes the less, and should therefore be learnt by every candidate for oratorical honours.

Some details of training must now be considered. In the first place it may be pointed out that whilst practice in singing is best conducted in *mezza voce*, in speaking exercise the voice should generally be used at its loudest. Articulation must be practised with the most laborious care and untiring patience, for a speaker who pronounces badly is like a writer ignorant of grammar. First of all the vowel sounds must be thoroughly mastered so that they may be produced with perfect purity. "Take care of the vowels and the consonants will take care of them selves" is a maxim that is scarcely an exaggeration.

They should be uttered frequently with varying degrees of intensity, and in different ways in rapid succession one after the other, or prolonging the sound as long as the breath holds out. Each vowel should also be pronounced in combination with the various consonants. A very useful table of syllables and words for this kind of exercise is given by Hullah at the end of the little work to which I have more than once referred. It is a good plan to practise speaking as rapidly as may be consistent with perfect distinctness, and again in slowly measured tones. The student should practise conscientiously and with full devotion of his utmost faculty to his task, never slurring it over in a mechanical or half-hearted way. When the "dry bones" of speech have been thoroughly mastered, passages should be read aloud or declaimed once or twice a day, if possible always in the presence of a competent critic who will stop the speaker *flagrante delicto* and make him see the error of his ways there and then.

SECTION IV.

Removal of Defects.

Defects of utterance can be cured only if the cause is recognized. For stammering nothing can be done unless the sufferer can learn to use his breath properly. The instructor's efforts must be mainly directed to teaching his pupil to acquire some degree of control over his diaphragm and other respiratory muscles, so that the air or motive power shall not be allowed to leak away before the vocal apparatus can be got ready for it. With persevering drill and ceaseless practice the two movements can be to a certain degree harmonized and co-ordinated, but it is to be feared the cure can seldom be complete, as an act which should be automatic is sure to be less perfectly done when it has to be performed with conscious effort. For stuttering it is questionable whether there is any radical or permanent remedy except in the slighter cases.

Much improvement, however, can be effected by an experienced teacher who will take the trouble to trace his pupil's difficulty to its source. In cases where the larynx is at fault the breathing must be attended to, and when the tongue is the peccant part the treatment must be directed to it. Various plans have at different times been proposed, and each has of course been vaunted by its inventor as infallible, and of universal application. Experience, however, has taught most of us that no remedy whatever is infallible, and it may be gathered from what has just been said that in the treatment of stuttering no single plan can be successful in all cases. Want of space prevents my doing more than allude in a general way to the different methods that have been suggested. They group themselves into *gymnastic* and *mechanical* measures. The aim of the former is to make the pupil acquire a proper control over his organs of speech by means of regulated exercise of the breathing apparatus and of the tongue, whilst the latter seeks to help him by means of instruments which serve to hold up or keep down the tongue.

All or most of these plans succeed fairly well for a time when the pupil is sustained by the encouragements of an enthusiastic master. It is too often the case, however, that when the cure is complete and the unfortunate sufferer is left to himself, disaster overtakes him, like the swimmer who has never learnt to buoy himself without corks. Nevertheless, I do not deny that great amelioration may be produced by rational and persevering treatment directed to the mental as well as to the physical constitution of the patient. I am inclined to consider a good deal of what is usually called "impediment" in speech to be due rather to weakness of volitional impulse than to any inherent defect in the structure or working of the organs. The will is there, but its behests are either imperfectly conveyed or blunderingly executed. In one of the worst cases of stuttering that I have met, the utterance was always improved by small doses of strychnia, whilst the sufferer was almost deprived of the power of speech by tobacco.[1] I think it probable that the utterance would be improved if the voice were always used in a loud key; the greater effort required for its production tending to ensure stronger

[1] Strychnia is a powerful stimulant of the nervous system whilst tobacco is a mild sedative.

and more harmonious action of the muscular apparatus.

Stammerers and stutterers should carefully avoid each other's company, and children of markedly nervous temperament should on no account be allowed to associate with persons who have any impediment or even singularity of speech. We read that the eloquent Basil acquired such an ascendency over the minds of his young hearers that they strove to copy his very appearance and manner of speaking. The same thing is said to have taken place at Oxford when Cardinal Newman occupied the pulpit of St. Mary's.

Unconscious mimicry is natural to most children, and to many adults. Tricks ot look and speech can be "caught," as every one knows. I know people so impressionable that one can tell by slight touches of brogue when they have been in Ireland or Scotland for a few weeks. Married couples often acquire a certain likeness to each other in the expression of the countenance from living long together. In cases of nervous disease like chorea, and especially hysteria, imitation conscious or unconscious is often so powerful a factor that no girl subject to such attacks should ever be allowed to remain in a boarding school. Taking this activity of the imitative faculty into consideration, it will be evident that nothing could be worse than to allow children to be much with stutterers or defective speakers of any kind.

It does not lie within the scope of the present

treatise to describe the means of remedying the various diseases and deformities which have been briefly indicated as affecting the articulation. Cleft palate can be cured in the young by a surgical operation, whilst in older subjects it may be palliated by wearing a plate (technically called an obturator) which fills up the gap. Enlarged tonsils,[1] growths in the larynx or in the post-nasal space, polypi, or extreme thickening of the mucous membrane covering the spongy bones, should be removed; deviation of the septum should be corrected; glandular enlargements under the tongue must be treated *secundum artem.* A long uvula must be shortened if it give rise to real inconvenience by trailing on the back of the tongue or hanging into the larynx, causing continual irritation, coughing, and even sickness. There is much misconception not only in the public mind but in the medical profession itself as to surgical curtailment of this little appendage. Whilst some look upon the operation as a *panacea* for every malady that can affect the throat, others regard it with equally fanatical dislike, as if the uvula were an organ of such importance that every atom of its structure must be considered sacred. The truth lies as usual between these two extremes, and whilst I am

[1] All sorts of mysterious sympathies have been supposed to exist between these troublesome little glands and remote organs, so that the removal of them is often looked upon with much apprehension. The only effect which I have ever observed on the voice, as well as on the health generally, from this operation has been of a beneficial nature.

utterly opposed to cutting the uvula or any other pare of the body "only for wantonness," I do not hesitate to remove a piece of it when it is evidently a source of continual discomfort. It will be noticed that I speak only of partial amputation ; the whole of the uvula should never be removed. Such a mutilation has a distinctly injurious effect on the voice, as the closure of the posterior opening of the nose is rendered difficult and often imperfect. The want of teeth must be supplied by artificial ones, which should be thoroughly well-fitted to the jaw. Many persons have an objection praiseworthy enough in itself to anything "false," but the necessity of repairing the ravages of time or disease in the case of teeth is entirely beyond all consideration of mere vanity. A man *must* have teeth if he wishes either to speak or to eat properly. I may be allowed to repeat, for the benefit of my readers, a word of caution to all wearers of artificial teeth; they should never fail to remove them before going to sleep. "Clergyman's sore throat" is a condition that is largely dependent on a wrong mode of producing the voice, and over-use of it, particularly if intermittent, has the same effect. Clergymen are by no means the only sufferers; school-teachers, reading-companions, hawkers, and others, are not less subject to the complaint. Hullah[1] tries to prove from the rarity of the disease among actors that it is due rather to too little than to too much exercise of the vocal mechanism. But, in

[1] *Op. cit.* p. 21.

the first place, few actors can have to speak for so long as two hours in any one evening, whereas that is I conceive, rather under, than over, the average time during which a clergyman has to use his voice *almost continuously* on Sundays. Then in the case of teachers, the drudgery of the work must be taken into account, the voice having to be used amidst various noises and depressing surroundings, often to dull and inattentive listeners. Speaking under such circumstances is an altogether different thing from speaking on the stage where everything helps to stimulate and excite, where applause nerves to fresh effort, and the very passion of acting, simulated though it be, produces for the time at least insensibility to fatigue. The difference is as great as that between an overworked cab-hack and a racehorse.

The treatment of "clergyman's sore throat" must be left in the hands of the physician, who, however, can accomplish little unless the sufferer desists from using his voice for some time. In most cases also the sufferer must afterwards go through a course of instruction in the art of voice-production. The dryness of the throat which is often felt as a distressing symptom by such patients can be alleviated by keeping a glycerine or chlorate of potash[1] lozenge, or (in imitation of a certain celebrated curate) an "acidulated drop" in the mouth. In addition to the emollient

[1] Wyeth's "compressed tablets" of chlorate of potash are especially convenient for this purpose, as they are so small that they can be held in the mouth whilst using the voice.

effect of the remedy, the mere presence of the foreign body promotes the secretion of fluid from the mucous membrane.

Another condition less familiarly known to the public and less chronic in character, but scarcely less distressing, is what Mandl[1] called *Fatigue de la Voix*. There is no particular disease in the vocal organs except perhaps a certain degree of congestion and relaxation, but there is a sense of weakness and inability to sound the voice, which sometimes gives way altogether. When the speaker does succeed in producing it, it is unsteady and deficient in volume, and the effort is most fatiguing, not merely to the organs immediately concerned, but to the general system. The mental distress is sometimes very great, the speaker being in an agony of terror lest his voice should fail him, a state of mind which must of course hasten the catastrophe. A still more severe degree of this disorder is what may be called "vocalist's cramp," in which the muscles from over-use lose the power of contracting (like an india rubber cord that has been overstretched), or can act only in an irregular and spasmodic way independently of the will or even contrary to it. Analogous conditions are often seen in other parts which have been overtaxed, as for instance in the muscles of the hand in persons who write much (scrivener's palsy), or in the muscles of accommodation in the eye in those whose

[1] *Hygiène de la Voix, parlée ou chantée*, 2nd edition, Paris, 1879, p. 1.

M

work obliges them to look intently at small objects, especially by artificial light. In cases of "fatigue of the voice," the chief remedy is absolute rest of the parts which have been overused; without this all medication is useless. Proper treatment can, however, help greatly in expediting the cure and making it more complete and durable, but it would be useless to refer to this subject further without entering into details which would be out of place in a popular treatise. The patient can greatly aid the doctor by avoiding whatever is likely to delay the cure, such as premature or injudicious use of the voice, overwork of any kind whether of body or mind, and quack remedies which are either inert or, worse still, productive of a passing benefit which is dearly bought by subsequent reaction. Among the principal hindrances to recovery I must place nervous impatience, anxiety, and fidgetiness, which the sufferer must struggle against with all his might. With time and perseverance I am convinced that no case of this kind is incurable, and if sufferers can be brought really to believe this, such faith will of itself tend to move the mountain of their complaint.

Amongst other aids which the patient can employ for himself I may mention friction and mechanical support to the larynx. A good way of applying the former is to sponge the parts round the Adam's Apple with tepid water, and afterwards with cold water mixed with a little vinegar or *Eau-de-Cologne*. This should be done for a few minutes, and the skin should then be thoroughly dried by rubbing it with a rough towel as hard as can be borne. Some slight manipulations may also be practised, such as kneading the sides of the larynx lightly and pushing it up and down with the fingers. It must be understood that these manœuvres should not be at all violent but they should be strong enough to be felt in the deeper parts of the neck. The larynx may also be steadied when one has to speak, either with the fingers or with some sort of mechanical support, *e.g.* an elastic belt with two little pads to press gently but firmly on the sides of the organ. A band fitted up with a small apparatus which sends a weak current of electricity constantly through the affected muscles may be worn round the neck with advantage. It is most important, however, that this should never be done except with the sanction of a competent professional adviser, and care must be exercised in selecting a suitable apparatus, as too many things of the sort are mere toys or worse. It must be remembered also that even genuine instruments need a great deal of attention, and some skill to keep them in working order.

A course of waters at Aix les Bains is likely to be of great use in cases of chronic congestion and relaxation of the vocal organs, whilst the Mont Dore "cure" is especially valuable as a protective against the tendency to winter catarrh, which is an unfailing characteristic of weak or over-worked throats.

SECTION V.

Special Hygiene for Speakers.

The hygienic rules which have already been laid down for singers apply with equal force to speakers. The sounder the condition of the body generally, the better will the voice be, especially for prolonged effort. All the things which have already been mentioned as likely to cause irritation to the delicate lining membrane of the throat must be avoided, and no trouble must be spared in acquiring the art of using the voice in the best way. That is indeed the very cornerstone of vocal hygiene without which all other things are practically useless. It is obvious that the least strain will be put upon the organs when the voice is confined to the middle of its compass, that is, when the tones are easiest and most natural to the speaker. The individual's own sensations are, within certain limits, the safest guide as to this, but they are by no means infallible, and nowhere is the skill of a competent teacher more clearly seen than in his power of helping his pupils to discover their *natural* tone of voice

In using the voice the speaker must be careful to put himself in the position most favourable for the free play of his vocal organs. An actor may be obliged by the dramatic fitness of things to speak in constrained attitudes just as he may have to disguise his voice, to stutter, or to lisp, but a preacher or orator has no excuse for using his voice otherwise than to the best advantage. The body should be held erect, but not stiffly like a soldier standing at "attention," the head well up, the chest expanded, the neck not compressed by tight scarves or collars of the garotting type so much affected by the *haute gomme* of the hour. If a man has to read, the book or paper should be held before him so as to be legible without bending the head till the chin almost touches the breast-bone, as is often the case. The voice must be, as it were, *thrown* at the most distant part of the audience, and the speech should be addressed mainly to those within compass of such range of vision as is possible without turning the body altogether to one side or the other. The orator should remember that nature *os homini sublime dedit*, and he should look his audience in the face. He should not speak with his eyes cast down unless as a rhetorical artifice in the way familiar to the astute Ulysses, who as we are told put on an appearance of modesty and hesitation in beginning to speak, the more effectually to conciliate his hearers. And indeed there is no surer way of securing silence and attention at the outset than to commence in such a key that the audience must "stand fixt to hear," and it may be added that such initial moderation will make the voice last longer. A man who has to speak for a considerable time must husband his resources as runners do in the early part of a race.

Broue[1] lays it down as a rule that the most absolute silence must be observed during the whole day before using the voice in the evening. This "counsel of perfection" is of course for actors, but if the rule is sound it must apply to speakers of all kinds. I do not consider that such an ultra-Trappistical code is beneficial, even supposing that any one could be found to adhere scrupulously to it. That the voice should not be *exerted* as in prolonged declamation or even much speaking in noisy streets, cabs, or trains, is what every one will agree to; but absolute silence would, I think, be rather injurious than otherwise.

I need not repeat here what has already been said on the subject of medicinal aids to the voice. Every public speaker has his own specific, from the Spartan glass of water to possets and concoctions of greater or less complexity of composition and considerable alcoholic strength. As there is hardly anything which hygienists have not condemned as pernicious to health in some way, even the glass of water has not escaped anathema. Few lecturers, however, would, I imagine, care to face an audience unsupported by the sight at least of the familiar fluid. In this matter, as already said, every experienced person must be a law unto himself. But I am bound to say that I consider the example of a leading actress (whose retirement has recently robbed English dramatic art of one of its most fascinating exponents) is one not to be rashly

[1] *Hygiène Philosophique des Artistes dramatiques*, Paris, 1836, p. 250.

followed by less gifted individuals. This lady is, or rather was, in the habit of drinking a glass of *iced* water immediately before going on the stage. To say nothing of the immediate shock to the nerves of the throat, the reaction that must inevitably follow such an application would be likely in less exceptional organisations to induce a degree of congestion that would seriously interfere with clearness of delivery. It cannot be repeated too often or with too much emphasis that all such violent measures (for such they are when applied to a part so delicately sensitive as the throat), even whilst appearing to give temporary relief are to be reprobated as entailing subsequent discomfort and possibly even disease. Another powerful argument against such things is the danger that after some time the speaker may become unable to dispense with them.

Sedatives may be necessary beforehand to subdue that excessive excitement which is common enough even in the most practised speakers, and which may reach such a degree as to make them incapable of doing full justice to themselves. I have already spoken of the beneficial effects in such cases of a tonic or sedative draught taken shortly before speaking; the great physiologist and surgeon, John Hunter, could never address even an audience of students without such a preparatory potion. Special care is necessary *after* speaking not to expose the throat to cold air on leaving the theatre or hall; the parts are then in a state of congestion from exercise which renders them very liable to become inflamed by a comparatively trifling cause. A good meal should follow any prolonged vocal effort, but hot or pungent things, which as already said are *always* hurtful, must be particularly avoided under such circumstances for the reason just given. In fact all the precautions which I have enjoined in various parts of this work against atmospheric or other irritants (close rooms, tobacco smoke, &c.,) are doubly necessary when the throat is congested and fatigued after a great effort.

Section VI.

Concluding Remarks.

In bringing this little work to a conclusion I must again draw the reader's attention to the fact that I have throughout been speaking purely as a physician. I have no desire or pretension to usurp the functions of the singing-master or elocutionist, nor do I claim any power of "endowing with artistic merit" voices which nature has made harsh and disagreeable. My aim has been to furnish the vocalist and public speaker with a guide to the *diseases* of the voice, and the best means of avoiding them. I am aware that the rules which I have laid down cannot be always strictly followed in practice nor is it perhaps altogether desirable that they should. No one, except perhaps Dr. Richardson, leads an ideally healthy life; even the members of the Sanitary and National Health

Societies would I have no doubt be individually found wanting if weighed in the balance of a severe hygiene. Thackeray observes that a doctor who has written a book on diet is almost always a *bon vivant*, and at medical symposia one is pretty sure to be edified by seeing authorities on gout and obesity showing an utter disregard of their own austere precepts. But in addition to the "touch of nature" which makes the divorce between principle and practice so familiar to weak humanity, a nobler feeling may sometimes be at the bottom of such revolts against hygienic dogma. It is a reaction, perhaps unconscious, against the wave of sanitarian fanaticism which is sweeping away one after the other nearly all the pleasures and much of the beauty of our poor mortal life. It is beginning to be forgotten that health, best gift of fortune though it be, is not an end in itself, but a means to the aecomplishment of whatever useful or noble work we have to do in the world. Mere health would be too dearly bought by the sacrifice of everything that makes life worth having. No man can be a hero who guides his footsteps solely by the light of a cautious hygiene; on the contrary he must often act in defiance of its dictates. But the most heroic bosom will find its generous throbbings dulled by improper nourishment, and sickness impairs the usefulness of the most energetic worker. Like the hero, the vocal artist must spend and be spent if he would achieve greatness. As Rousseau said of cloistered virtue, a voice which can be kept in order only by a strict observance of hygienic laws is hardly worth the trouble of preserving.

The man who puts the question of his own physical well-being before everything else can never excel except as a valetudinarian. But whilst thus alluding to an element of weakness in the modern gospel of health,[1] I must not be understood as wishing to undervalue its teaching. It is well for the most daring sailor to know the rocks on which his ship may split and all the manifold dangers of the sea, not that through fear of them he may spend his life in inglorious ease on shore, but that his very courage and skill may not lead him to premature destruction. So it is with vocalists. Hygiene tells them what is likely to injure or ruin the voice; it rests with each one to decide for himself what risks he shall run for the sake of art or fame or livelihood. I have attempted to set forth as lucidly as possible the general principles of voice preservation and the most important points of practical detail; the individual application must be left to those whom it immediately concerns. Though it is only drawing-room tenors that may need all the precautions of a hot-house hygiene, even the most richly endowed organization cannot long defy natural laws with impunity.

[1] Summarised in Lord Beaconsfield's electioneering parody of the Preacher, *Sanitas Sanitatum et omnia Sanitas.*

APPENDIX I.

ANATOMY OF THE VOCAL ORGANS.

ALTHOUGH a knowledge of anatomy will not make a bad singer a good one, a slight acquaintance with the structure of his instrument will help him to keep it in working order. The motive power or air-blast which sets the vocal cords in vibration is supplied by the lungs. These are two sponge-like organs roughly conical in shape, the lower end or "base" being downwards, whilst the upper, or "apex," rises slightly up into the neck behind the collar-bone. Together with the heart they fill the cavity of the chest. The structure of the lung will be better apprehended on tracing the path taken by the *inspired* air downwards from the larynx.[1] When it has passed below the level of the Adam's apple it enters the trachea or windpipe. This is a short tube running straight down from the larynx into the chest, at the

[1] The arrows in the Frontispiece indicate the direction taken by the *expired* air whether in the act of breathing or in sounding the voice.

upper part of which it divides into two smaller tubes ("bronchi"), which branch off from the main trunk at an obtuse angle (see Fig. 14, *br*), and run in a slanting direction downwards and outwards, one to each lung. As they approach those organs they begin to break up into still smaller tubes, and this subdivision goes on within the lung itself till the ultimate ramifications end in tiny pouches or "air-cells," which the unscientific reader may picture to his mind's eye as resembling soap-bubbles of infinitesimal size. Each "bubble," or cluster of "bubbles," communicates through a minute opening with the ultimate divisions of the bronchial tubes. The walls of these little cells are very thin and of highly elastic structure, and in the substance of each is a delicate network of very small blood-vessels, called "capillaries." It is here that the vital part of the respiratory process, viz. the purification of the blood, takes place. This consists essentially in an exchange of gases between the blood and the air, whereby the former yields up the waste matters of the system in the form of carbonic acid, receiving in return a fresh supply of oxygen. It is evident from this how important it is to have a sufficient supply of pure air, *i.e.* air which contains its due proportion of oxygen, to renovate the blood. A room in which a number of people are sitting soon becomes "close" if the windows and doors are kept shut: this indicates that the oxygen in the air is exhausted, its place being taken by carbonic acid exhaled from the lungs of the assembly, so that the purification of the blood must necessarily become more and more imperfect. This process of re-breathing air that has already been used, if long continued, leads to asphyxia and death, but short of this point it gives rise to much distress, and even disease. This cause, for instance, lies at the root of much so-called "delicacy," susceptibility to cold, languor, headache, and nervous depression.

It is not so much, however, the physiological as the mechanical part of breathing that I am immediately concerned with. Besides their principal function of purifying the blood, the lungs are the bellows of the vocal instrument. They propel a current of air up the windpipe to the narrow chink of the larynx, which throws the membranous edges or lips ("vocal cords") of that organ into vibration, and thereby produces sound. The air taken into the lungs in inspiration distends the air-cells; it is driven out again mainly by the contraction of the elastic walls of the little cells themselves. This is the essential feature of the expiratory act. Inspiration, on the other hand, is more complex, and may be performed in two or three different ways or by a combination of them. They all have the common object of increasing the capacity of the chest so as to leave room for the expansion of the lungs as the air is drawn into them. What may be termed the natural method of breathing is performed principally by the agency of a large muscle known as the diaphragm (Frontispiece, *l*, and

Fig. 14, *d*), which spreads across the cavity of the trunk, dividing it into an upper or thoracic, and a lower or abdominal, space. The former is known as the chest; the latter (to ears polite) as the "stomach." The diaphragm, when in a state of repose, arches upwards, so as to make the floor of the chest a

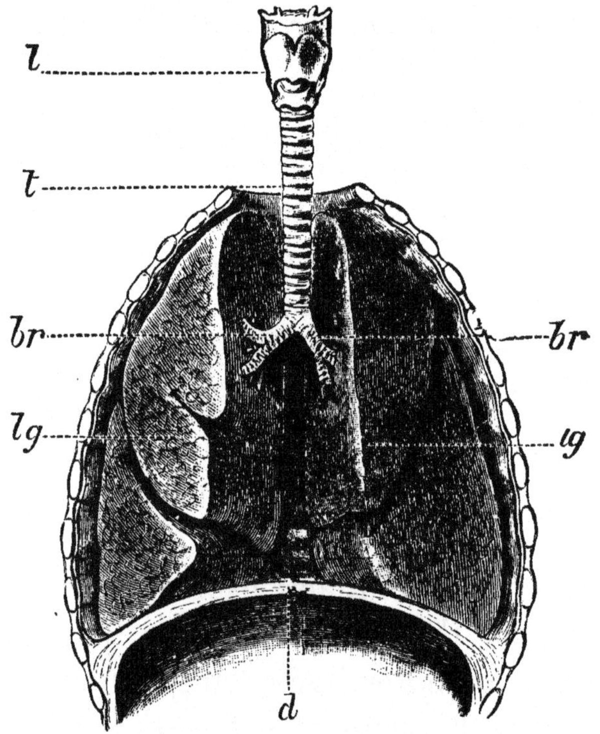

FIG. 14.—THE VOCAL INSTRUMENT.
l, larynx; *t*, trachea: *br*, bronchi; *lg*, lung; *d*, diaphragm.

kind of dome, on the convexity of which rest the bases of the lungs, whilst the under surface looks towards the abdomen. In contracting, the muscle descends towards the latter cavity so as to make the floor of the chest almost flat, thus leaving room for the increase in volume of the inflated lungs. In expiration the diaphragm simply returns to its former condition. This mode of breathing is known as "*diaphragmatic.*" The action of the diaphragm is assisted by the elevation and partial expansion of the ribs (see Fig. 14), which, together with the breast-bone, make a cage-like framework for the chest. Each pair of ribs is furnished with two sets of muscular fibres which act on them in contrary directions. Breathing carried on mainly by the ribs is called "*costal*" respiration, and it is sometimes largely practised by women with the upper ribs alone owing to the partial fixation of the lower by tight stays. In very violent breathing the collar-bone (or "clavicle") is forcibly drawn up by the muscles of the neck so as to assist the action of those which act on the ribs. This method of inspiration is called "*clavicular.*" These three modes of inspiration include all the means at our disposal for taking breath, and it is important for all who use the voice to understand them. Clavicular breathing is seldom employed except in certain diseased conditions and during very violent exertion.[1] To obtain its full power the hands must firmly hold some fixed object in order that the collar-bone may (through the shoulder-blade) have a fulcrum. When costal or diaphragmatic breathing is spoken of, it

[1] The force with which the clavicle may be drawn up is shown by the fact related by Dr. Walshe (*Dramatic Singing*, London, 1881, p. 15, footnote), that Rubini actually broke his collar-bone in delivering a very high note.

must always be remembered that in the normal human body both methods are always used together, the one assisting and completing the other. The terms are in reality relative, and are, or should be, applied only as one or the other type predominates in an individual at a given time.

The larynx is sometimes absurdly called the "voice-box," as if it were one of those ingenious toys which grind out a thin strain of wiry melody on being wound up. If a comparison is necessary, I should prefer to liken it to a hollow wedge, of which the sharp end looks forward. The larynx is, in fact, an expansion of the upper part of the trachea, on which it is placed like a funnel on the top of a tube. The large end, which is uppermost, is provided with a self-acting lid, whilst the lower is continuous with the windpipe, and through it with the lungs. Almost round at its lower end, the larynx is nearly triangular in shape at its upper opening, the apex, of course, being in front. The walls are formed mostly by pieces of cartilage of various size and shape held together by muscles and other soft tissues, the whole being covered by a smooth, moist integument like the skin lining the mouth, and known as "mucous membrane." The lowest cartilage, *i.e.* the one immediately above the windpipe, is called the "cricoid" (Fig. 15, *cc*), and is almost circular in outline. In shape it resembles a signet ring, the broad surface (representing the seal) being at the back. It is usually large enough in circumference to admit a man's forefinger. Above the cricoid is the "thyroid" or buckler cartilage (Fig. 15, *tc*) which forms the front and sides of the larynx. It consists of two lateral parts or "wings" which are joined together in front at an acute angle, forming a prominence which is visible in the neck as the "Adam's apple." A notch varying

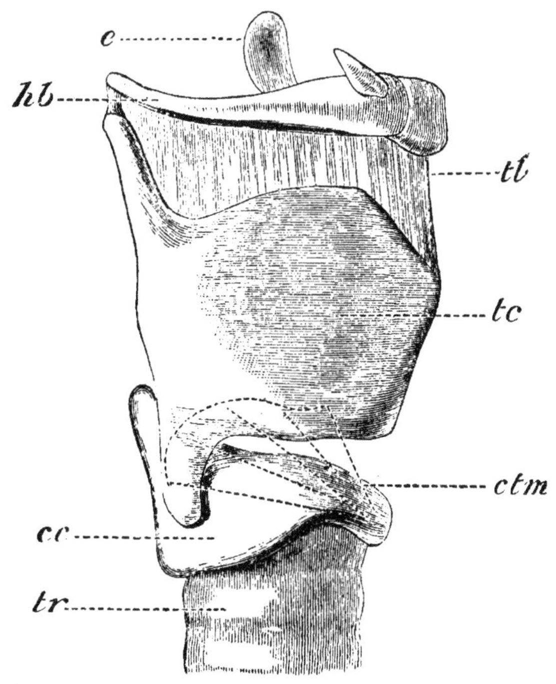

FIG. 15.—LATERAL VIEW OF THE FRAMEWORK OF THE LARYNX AND HYOID BONE (SEEN FROM THE OUTSIDE.)

e, epiglottis; *hb*, byo'd bone; *tl*, thyro-hyoid ligament; *tc*, thyroid cartilage *cc*, cricoid cartilage; *ctm*, crico-thyroid muscle; *tr*, trachea.

in depth in different individuals, but usually more marked in men than in women, separates the wings at the upper part of their angle of union. The wings are widely apart behind, and the hinder edge of each is prolonged upwards and downwards into little offsets, called respectively the upper and lower "horns." By the latter the thyroid is connected with the cricoid cartilage by means of a joint which permits a gliding movement of the one surface on the other. The "arytenoid" cartilages (Fig. 16, *ac*) are two small pyramidal bodies placed one at each side on the top of the cricoid behind. The base of

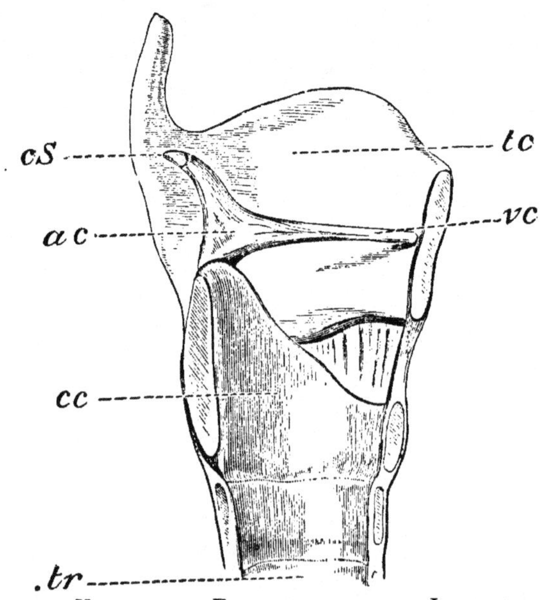

FIG. 16.—LATERAL VIEW OF THE FRAMEWORK OF THE LARYNX FROM WHICH THE EPIGLOTTIS HAS BEEN REMOVED. (SEEN FROM THE INSIDE.)

tc, thyroid cartilage; *ac*, arytenoid cartilage; *cS*, capitulum Santorini; *vc*, vocal cord; *cc*, cricoid cartilage; *tr*, trachea.

the pyramid rests on the cricoid (see Fig. 16), with which it articulates by a joint allowing free movement in various directions. The three corners of the base are directed inwards, outwards, and forwards, the two latter projections being of especial importance. The anterior process or spur is connected with the hinder extremity of the vocal cord, and is hence called the "vocal process," whilst the outer angle forms the lever-arm, by the aid of which most of the muscular movements belonging to the larynx itself are performed. Attached to the summit of the arytenoid cartilage is a little roundish piece of gristle, called after its discoverer *capitulum Santorini* (Fig. 16, *cS*), and further outwards in the fold of mucous membrane leading to the epiglottis is another similar nodule called the "cartilage of Wrisberg" (Fig. 5, *cW*) in honour of the anatomist who first described it. These little cartilaginous bodies serve to give strength to the membranous rim of the larynx, like the bits of whalebone and stout canvas which give stiffness to certain parts of a lady's dress.

Lastly there is the "epiglottis" (Fig. 15, *e*, and Fig. 17, *e*; see also the various laryngoscopic drawings, pp. 37-42), which is something like a leaf in shape, and is situated between the root of the tongue and the opening of the larynx; it forms a lid which is open so as to allow free passage to the air in breathing, but closes tightly down over the larynx in swallowing so that the food may pass backwards safely into the gullet (Fig. 18, *oe*; note also the tube behind the windpipe in Frontispiece.) The essential organ of voice is contained within the cavity enclosed by the cartilages just described; it consists of two membranous lips usually called vocal cords (Fig. 17, *rvc* and *lvc*, and Fig. 18, *vc*), which extend from the front to the back of the space. In front they are attached just behind the Adam's apple, *i.e.* to the inner part of the angle formed by the junction of the two wings of the thyroid cartilage, and behind to the anterior spur or "vocal process" (see Fig. 18, *vp*) of the arytenoid cartilage: the two cords

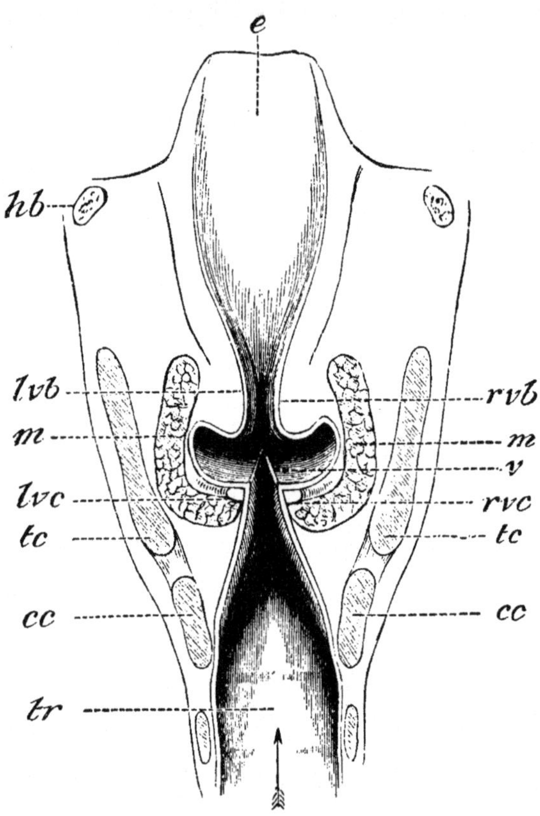

FIG. 17.—TRANSVERSE VERTICAL SECTION OF THE LARYNX. (FROM A FROZEN SECTION MADE BY DR. NORRIS WOLFENDEN.)

e, epiglottis; *hb*, hyoid bone; *lvb*, left ventricular band; *rvb*, right ventricular band: *m*, section of several muscles lying close together; *v*, ventricle or pouch of the larynx; *lvc*, left vocal cord; *rvc*, right vocal cord; *tc*, thyroid cartilage; *cc*, cricoid cartilage; *tr*, trachea.

are therefore close together in front and somewhat apart behind. Along the outer edge of each runs the thyro-arytenoid muscle (see Fig. 18), which is moreover firmly bound to the membrane by some of its own fibres. The space between the outer border of the muscle and the inner surface of the thyroid cartilage is padded with loose connective tissue (Fig. 18, *ct*), so that the vocal "cord" is not a *string*, but the free edge of a projecting fold of membrane (see Fig. 17, *rvc* and *lvc*). The upper part is broader than the rest, so that the inner edges project towards each other. They are made of fine elastic tissue mingled with a variable amount of fibrous material. Of course there are an infinite number of individual differences in the cords as regards length, thickness, elasticity, and other qualities just as there are in other parts of the body. The vocal cords with the arytenoid cartilages behind enclose a small space forming the opening of the air-passage and known as the "glottis" (Fig. 18), and the free edges of the vocal cords constitute *the lips of the glottis;* it is the vibration of these lips which produces the voice. The length of each cord or vocal lip is a trifle more than half an inch in men, and rather less than half an inch in women; the male glottis as a whole is very nearly an inch, and the female not quite three-fourths of an inch. Immediately above the vocal cord on each side is a little pocket or "ventricle" (Fig. 17, *v*), which is very variable in size, being sometimes a mere slit, whilst in other cases it is large enough to admit the point of the finger. The lower edge of this opening is formed by the vocal cord itself, whilst the upper consists of a narrow fringe of membrane, formerly known as the false cord, to which many years ago I gave the name of "ventricular band" (Fig. 17, *rvb* and *lvb*; see also the laryngoscopic drawings, pp. 37-42), now almost universally employed. The ventricular band is nothing more than the lower edge of a membranous fold stretching from the side of the epiglottis in front to the arytenoid cartilage behind and completing the side wall of the upper portion of the larynx. These parts form the framework of the organ; it only remains to describe the muscles which pull the cartilages and the cords towards or away from each other, and thus produce the wonderful variety of quality, tone, and intensity of voice with which every one is familiar even in the ordinary speech of his own limited circle of friends. The laryngeal muscles are small fleshy slips, attached at each end to different parts of the framework which, by the contraction, *i.e.* shortening of their fibres, are drawn nearer to each other. Thus there is a muscle ("crico-thyroid") (Fig. 15, *ctm*) at each side, which runs backwards and upwards from the cricoid cartilage to the lower edge, and adjoining horn of the thyroid cartilage. Another muscle ("arytenoid") passes at the back of the larynx from one arytenoid cartilage to the other. A third muscle ("posterior crico-arytenoid") stretches from the back or signet of the cricoid cartilage to the outer spur of the arytenoid. Between the same point of the last-named body, and the upper part of the *side* of the cricoid passes a small muscle ("lateral crico-arytenoid"). A fleshy bundle ("thyro-arytenoid") (Fig. 18) passes from the back of the thyroid cartilage just below the attachment of the vocal cords horizontally backwards to the arytenoid cartilage. This important muscle lies immediately to the outer side of the membranous portion of

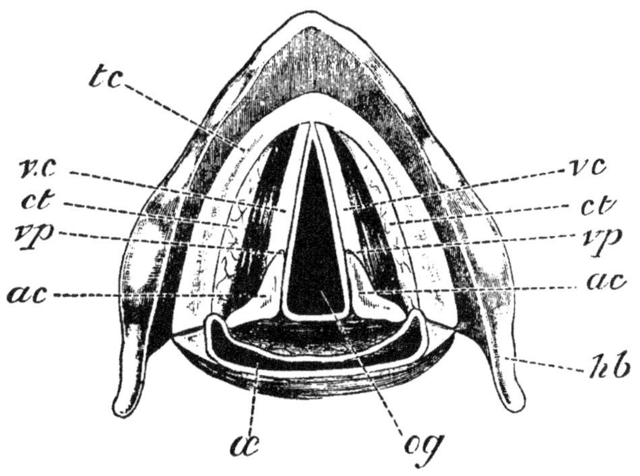

FIG. 18.—THE GLOTTIS, WITH ITS SURROUNDING PARTS DISSECTED. (SEEN FROM ABOVE.)

tc, thyroid cartilage; *vc*, the vocal cords; *ct*, connective tissue between the cord and the wall of the larynx; *vp*, vocal process or anterior spur of the arytenoid cartilage; *ac*, arytenoid cartilage; *æ*, œsophagus; *hb*, hyoid bone; *og*, orifice of the glottis. The dark lines running parallel to the lip of the glottis (between *vc* and *ct*) represent the fibres of the thyro-arytenoid muscle.

the vocal cord, to which it gives bulk and solidity. Its fibres have a very complicated arrangement, some being attached to the arytenoid cartilage, some to the fold between that point and the epiglottis, and some also, as has been recently shown,[1] to the substance of the vocal lips themselves. The muscle is, in fact, attached to the vocal cord all the way

[1] Shattock, *Journ. Anat. and Phys.* vol. xvi. p. 485; 1882. Mr. Shattock's dissections were undertaken at the suggestion of Professor Garcia.

along, just as the muscles which move the mouth, nostrils, and eyes, are attached not only to the points which it is their function to draw together, but likewise to the skin of the face between those features, thus giving the countenance its mobility and almost infinite variety of expression. The last muscle requiring mention is the depressor of the epiglottis which is attached to the arytenoid cartilage, and to the corresponding lateral margin of the epiglottis.

The action of these various muscles is excessively complicated, and any one who should be able fully and exactly to describe it, would dispel the mystery which still surrounds the whole subject of voice-production. I can only allude briefly in this place to a few points that appear incontestable. Thus, the vocal cords are *stretched* by the contraction of the crico-thyroids,[1] *relaxed* by that of the thyro-arytenoids,

[1] A glance at Fig. 15, *ctm*, will show that the muscle does not act *directly* on the vocal cord, but on the cartilages to which it is attached. It used to be believed that the effect was produced by pulling the thyroid cartilage down so as to increase the distance between it and the arytenoid cartilage behind, and thus *stretch* the vocal cord by moving one of its points of attachment further away from the other. It is now known that it is the cricoid cartilage which is pulled upwards at its front part. Owing to its circular shape this entails the lowering of the other portion of its circumference, which necessarily drags with it the arytenoid cartilage and the posterior attachment of the vocal cord, which is thereby put on the stretch. This mode of action of the crico-thyroid muscle, though long ago propounded as a *guess* by a stray anatomist or two, has now been experimentally *proved* by Dr. F. H. Hooper, of Boston, U.S. (*Trans. Amer. Laryngol. Assoc.* New York, 1883; p. 118 *et seq.*). He

whilst they are *approximated* by the lateral, and *separated* by the posterior crico-arytenoids. When, however, these latter muscles act in combination with the others, they also play the part of "tensors." By the arytenoid muscle the cartilages of that name are drawn towards each other, so as to lessen or even close the chink of the glottis at its posterior part. Lastly, the epiglottis is drawn by its depressor muscle over the upper opening of the larynx. There are other muscles which need not be more particularly described here which draw the larynx as a whole up or down; the action of these, though important, is only auxiliary in voice-production.

We now come to the third element in the vocal apparatus, viz. the parts which give resonance to the voice. The lungs supply the air-blast or power, and thereby regulate the *intensity* of the sound; the rate of vibration of the vocal lips governs the *pitch*, whilst the resonance-chambers give the voice its peculiar quality or *timbre*. Taking the resonance-chambers *seriatim*, there is first the cavity of the *chest* bound round, as already stated, by the ribs covered with thick folds of muscle, a layer of fat of variable

shows conclusively that two factors are concerned in the tension of the vocal cords; first, the crico-thyroid muscle in the way just described; secondly, the air-blast itself, which, by its impact against the lips of the glottis, carries the whole larynx somewhat upwards. The cricoid cartilage, however, moves relatively more than the thyroid, and consequently is brought up close to it in front, a movement which, as has already been seen, has the effect of stretching the vocal cord.

thickness, and the skin as side walls, and with the diaphragm as floor (Fig. 15, *d*). The shape of the chest as a whole is conical, the lower part being the widest. In the cavity, besides the lungs and the lower part of the windpipe with its branches, is the heart, with large blood-vessels issuing from and emptying themselves into it. The heart lies between the lungs, and behind it the gullet, or food-tube, passes downwards to the stomach. If the hand is placed on the chest whilst a deep note is being sounded, its walls can be felt to vibrate strongly.

Immediately above the vocal cords is another resonance-chamber, known as the "supraglottic space of the larynx" (Fig. 17, above the level of *rvc* and *lvc*). This is, in fact, the upper part of the funnel-shaped cavity already described, and is bounded bv the membrane extending between the sides of the epiglottis and the peaks of the arytenoid cartilages, and the epiglottis itself. These parts may come together, so as almost entirely to cover the glottis, or may remain wide apart. Above the larynx altogether is a space, known as the "pharynx," which extends to the base of the skull and opens into the mouth, and, higher up, communicates with the back of the nose by two passages called the "posterior nares" (see Frontis piece). The walls of the pharynx being for the most part muscular are highly contractile; the dimensions and shape of the cavity are, therefore, susceptible of very great modification in every individual. Then there is the mouth, which is separated from the nasal chambers by the hard palate, the latter thus forming at once the roof of the mouth and the floor of the nose. From the hinder part of the hard palate the soft palate, or "velum," hangs down like a curtain over the root of the tongue. The soft palate has a small appendage of variable length, projecting like a tongue from the middle of its lower edge; this is the "uvula" (Frontispiece, *uf*), the *bête noire* of many vocalists, who look upon it as the root of all evil as far as the throat is concerned. The soft palate and uvula are composed almost entirely of muscular tissue covered by the usual mucous membrane. The curtain consequently lengthens or shortens as occasion may require, and is sometimes retracted in the same way that the finger of a glove is accidentally drawn in when the glove is being taken off the hand.

Although the uvula is not as a rule under the direct government of the will, it may by assiduous practice be made partially submissive thereto. When at rest the uvula hangs vertically down, and as the tongue bulges upwards at its posterior part a sort of valve is formed, which shuts off the cavity of the mouth from the pharynx. In respiration the natural course of the indrawn air is through the nose, down the pharynx, into the windpipe. In swallowing, however, the valve just referred to is opened by the separation of the tongue from the soft palate, the latter being drawn up so as to touch the back wall of the pharynx, and cut off all communication with the nose. This closure is rendered more complete by a slight projection of the pharyngeal wall in the middle line behind. To this the edge of the updrawn soft palate is applied, the back and sides of the space being at the same time pressed towards each other by the fibres of the superior constrictor, a muscle which surrounds the upper part of the pharynx, and in contracting compresses the cavity as by the grasp of an encircling hand. Under these circumstances, it is obvious that the pressure of a column of air from below, *i.e.* in the direction of the laryngeal blast, serves only to tighten the naso-pharyngeal valve. All this machinery is governed by the will, so that the passage from the mouth to the nose can be cut off entirely or in part. The action of the soft palate, therefore, in singing and speaking, is of the most complex nature; indeed, the movements of this little body are even yet not perfectly understood, in spite of its being under such constant observation. I have, however, tried to give an intelligible account of what may be called its fundamental action as a naso-pharyngeal valve, and of the less vital but still important part which it plays as an imperfect pharyngo-buccal valve. It is necessary that this two-fold function of the soft palate should be thoroughly understood by the voice-trainer, as the muscles which move it can be educated just like those of any other part.

The "fauces" are sharply defined folds which project on each side of the interior of the throat. They are in reality prolongations of the lower edge of the soft palate, where it unites with the inner wall of the mouth. There are two ridges on each side, an anterior and a posterior one, which diverge from each other in a downward direction, like the letter V reversed (Λ); between them on each side lies the tonsil. The folds just described are technically known as the "pillars" of the fauces, whilst the part of the mouth bounded on each side by the tonsils, being the narrowest point of the cavity, is called the "isthmus." Each "pillar" incloses a bundle of muscular fibres; the front one (called *palato-glossus*) being connected with the under part of the side of the tongue, whilst the hinder one (*palato-pharyngeus*) runs much further down into the throat, and is attached in a rather complicated manner to the side of the pharynx and upper part of the larynx. It is obvious that, both these muscles acting as they do on the soft palate, the tongue and the larynx, must be most important factors in voice-production. The "tonsils" are small glandular bodies situated, as aforesaid, between the pillars of the fauces on each side. In the healthy state they are often so small or so deeply embedded in the groove formed by the folds in front of and behind them that they are almost invisible, whilst, on the other hand, when enlarged by disease they may project so far across as to touch each other in the middle line. Their intimate structure need not be described. To the naked eye they appear roundish bodies, about the size of half a hazel-nut, with a surface dimpled by depressions which are in reality the mouths of tiny channels leading from the interior of the gland and opening into the mouth. The use of the tonsils has never been discovered, nor so far as I know, even guessed at by the scientific imagination, though various superstitions concerning them are deeply rooted in the popular mind. Not many years ago a man of "leading" if not of "light" in the medical profession grounded a formidable indictment against the wisdom of the Creator, mainly on the existence of such purposeless excrescences.

The "nasal cavities" consist of two passages divided from each other by a vertical partition called the "septum." Each passage extends upwards almost as far as the base of the brain, from which indeed it is separated only by thin plates of bone, perforated with many holes like a sieve; through these apertures slender filaments (offsets of the first or olfactory nerve) pass, to terminate in the mucous membrane lining the upper third of the nasal chambers. It is accordingly in this portion of the nose that the sense of smell resides, the lower two-thirds of the cavity forming a channel for the air. For the purpose of warming this air before it reaches the lungs, what may be called a system of hot-water pipes is provided. From the outer wall of each nostril project three small curved osseous plates known from their structure as the *spongy bones* (Frontispiece, *c*). On these bones is arranged a close network of vessels, in such a way that a considerable quantity of blood is contained in a comparatively limited space. The air in passing over this collection of hot fluid is warmed to a degree that may be estimated by comparing the sensation which is caused at the back of the throat by a current of air drawn in directly through the mouth with that produced by air inspired through the nose. On either side of the nasal passage, and above it in front and behind are hollow spaces ("sinuses") in the neighbouring bones, all directly or indirectly communicating with the nose (see Frontispiece, *a* and *b*). The size of these cells varies much in different individuals, but it is obvious that in every one they must have a very great influence on the resonance and quality of the voice. A glance at the woodcut (Frontispiece) will enable the reader easily to understand the main features of the description just given.

The organs of *voice* having been described, those of *speech* must next be briefly referred to. Articulation is effected by the action of the palate, tongue, teeth, and lips, which, by the almost infinite variety of position which they assume relatively to each other, modify and break up the current of sound as it issues through the mouth into syllables and words. The palate has already been treated of in sufficient detail from the anatomical point of view. The tongue is a mass of muscle, the fibres of which cross each other in an extremely intricate manner. Its root is attached to the hyoid bone (Fig. 15, *hb*), which, as its name implies, resembles the Greek letter *υ*, and is placed horizontally in the throat a little way above the larynx, with the convex border in front, and two long processes ("greater cornua") pointing backwards. To the upper and lower edges of this little bone various muscles are attached, which pull it up or down, the larynx of course participating in each movement and rising or falling in the neck for an inch or two. The tongue is also attached by muscular fibres and connective tissue to the inner surface of the lower jaw in front and at the sides. The evil repute in which the tongue is held by moralists of the sterner sort is somewhat supported by anatomical evidence, for it is in reality a *double* organ, a vertical partition dividing it longwise into two equal parts. The mobility of the tongue of course varies extremely in different persons, and it may be cultivated to the extent of touching the tip of the nose, or, in other cases, of being passed backwards and upwards behind the soft palate[1] The "teeth" are thirty-two in number, sixteen in each jaw, but it is rare in modern life to find a complete set after the age of twenty-five or thirty. If too close together they give a peculiar indistinctness to the utterance, but if entirely wanting in front the articulation of certain letters becomes impossible: The lips need no description, but attention may be called to the fact that the substance of them is formed by muscular fibres arranged in circular bundles round the mouth; other fleshy slips connect the lips with the nose, the cheek, and the skin of the face. All these are liable to defects which may be corrected by appropriate training.

[1] This is the feat known as "swallowing the tongue," which is a favourite method of suicide with some negro races.

APPENDIX II.

CRITICAL OBSERVATIONS ON THE VARIOUS THEORIES AS TO THE MECHANISM OF THE REGISTERS.

The old Italian masters, who lived in blissful ignorance of the laryngoscope, recognised only two registers[1] of the human voice, the "chest" and the falsetto or "head," the two latter terms being exactly synonymous.[2] They of course spoke from what doctors call the purely *clinical* point of view, *i.e.* from the observation of voices in actual use,

[1] So called from the "registers" or different stops of the organ.

[2] See Tosi (*op. cit.* p. 15), and Mancini (*op. cit.* p. 43). Galliard, however, the English translator of Tosi, seems in a footnote to make a distinction between the "falsetto" and the "head" register. He says (in second edition, London, 1743, p. 22), "*Voce di petto* is a full voice, which comes from the breast by strength, and is the most sonorous and expressive; *di testa* comes more from the throat than from the breast, and is capable of more volubility. *Falsetto* is a feigned voice, which is entirely formed in the throat, has more volubility than any, but of no substance." There is no such differentiation of the falsetto from the head voice in Tosi's text.

without troubling themselves much as to how the difference was brought about. Johannes Müller, from the opposite standpoint of pure experiment on the larynx removed from the body, was also led to define two registers, the "chest" and "head."

The immediate effect of the invention of the laryngoscope was to throw the whole subject into almost hopeless confusion by the introduction of all sorts of errors of observation, each claiming to be founded on ocular proof, and believed in with corresponding obstinacy.

Garcia[1] divided the voice into "chest," "falsetto," and "head," all three being common to both sexes, but females having a greater range of "head," and men of "chest" notes. In each the chest and head registers were further subdivided into two parts. "upper" and "lower." Taking this view in connection with Garcia's own definition of a "register" as a "series of consecutive homogeneous sounds going from low to high, produced by the action of a certain mechanism," it is evident that he looks upon the singing voice as produced by five distinct mechanisms. Madame Seiler[2] followed Garcia in his arrangement of the registers, though differing from him as to certain details. Mr. Emil Behnke,[3]

[1] *Observations physiologiques sur la Voix humaine*, 1855, 2nd edition, Paris, 1861, p. 25 *et seq.*

[2] *The Voice in Singing;* Philadelphia, 1881, p. 53 *et seq.* (Mme. Seiler's views were first published in German in 1861.)

[3] *Mechanism of the Human Voice;* London, 1880, p. 71 *et seq.*

taking his classification from Madame Seiler and his nomenclature from Mr. Curwen,[1] prefers to parcel out the voice into a *thick* (chest), a *thin* (falsetto), and a *small* (head) register, the thick and the thin being each again subdivided into upper and lower, as in the Garcia-Seiler scheme. Mr. Behnke has been able[2] to indoctrinate with this view his *collaborateur* Mr. Lennox Browne, whose own formerly expressed opinions on the question, though somewhat hazy,[3] showed a leaning towards the more simple division into two registers. Dr. Wesley Mills[4] inclines to Madame Seller's arrangement of the registers, but pleads for a terminology that shall involve no theory as to production, but merely indicate relative pitch, *e.g.* lower, middle, and upper. Mandl,[5] who recognises only two registers, had already employed this system of nomenclature, calling the "chest" and "head" divisions "lower"

[1] *Teachers' Manual;* London, 1875, p. 173.

[2] *Voice, Song, and Speech,* 2nd edition; London, 1884, p. 163 *et seq.*

[3] *Medical Hints on the Production and Management of the Singing Voice,* 5th edition; London, 1877, p. 31 *et seq.*

[4] *An examination of some controverted points of the physiology of the voice, especially the registers of the singing voice and the falsetto.* Read before the American Association for the Advancement of Science at Montreal, August, 1882. Although in the main agreeing with Garcia and Madame Seiler, Dr. Mills, in a private letter to me, dated April 10th, 1884, says: "I don't know that I care to be set down as a hard and fast advocate of any division of the registers now adopted."

[5] *Hygiène de la Voix parlée ou chantée,* 2nd edition, Paris 1879, p. 37 *et seq.*

and "upper" respectively. Battaille,[1] Koch,[2] Vacher,[3] Martels,[4] together with Gouguenheim and Lermoyez,[5] also adhere to the two-register system.

Before proceeding to discuss the views of those writers in detail, it may be remarked that many singing-masters find a division into chest, middle or mixed, and head or falsetto, the most convenient for practical purposes.

This disagreement as to terms, however, is trifling, compared to the diversity of opinion as to facts which we find amongst rival authorities on voice-production. Lehfeldt[6] in the course of certain experiments on an exsected larynx, accidentally blew with less force than he intended, and thus produced some very high notes, the character of which reminded him of the sound of the flageolet. He jumped at once to the conclusion that he had discovered the secret of the falsetto voice, which he attributed to "want of force in the air-blast, which is too weak to throw the whole breadth of the cord into vibration." "I was," he continues, "led to this conclusion by the fact that whilst in the production of chest tones I could see the

[1] *Nouvelles Recherches sur la Phonation*, Paris, 1861, p. 67 *et seq.*

[2] *De la Voix humaine*, Luxembourg, 1874, p. 20.

[3] *De la Voix chez l'homme*, Paris, 1877, p. 29.

[4] *Physiologie de la Phonation. Revue bibl. univ. des Sciences Médicales*, t. ii. Nos. 13 and 15, 1885.

[5] *Physiologie de la Voix et du Chant*, Paris, 1885, p. 145 *et seq.*

[6] *Nonnulla de vocis formatione. Dissert. Inaug.* Berolini 1835, p. 58.

vibrations with a magnifying glass, I could not see them in the utterance of falsetto notes. Only the edges seemed to act."[1] But what kept the substance of the cord from vibrating? This puzzled our inquirer till he found that an old anatomist (Fabricius ab Aquapendente) had shown that certain fibres of the thyro-arytenoid muscle pass horizontally into the vocal cords, and Lehfeldt conjectured that by the contraction of these the vibration of the outer edge of the cord might be checked. It is evident that this hypothesis of Lehfeldt's rested on a very slender basis of observation, and it would probably have fallen into oblivion had it not been adopted by the great physiologist Müller, whose brilliant chapter on the voice has been the *locus canonicus* on which nearly all succeeding writers have founded their doctrines. The name of Lehfeldt (although duly mentioned by Müller) has been forgotten, and his view is almost invariably cited as that of Müller. The theory itself is accepted as true by most investigators, chiefly on the mere authority of its reputed author.

Garcia, from observation with the laryngoscope, asserts that in the lower part of the chest register the whole of the glottis is thrown into full loose vibrations, the vibrating edges including the anterior spur of the arytenoid cartilage, as well as the vocal band proper; as the pitch rises, however, the cartilages come into closer apposition, till the vibration is confined to the vocal cord. This sequence is repeated in the falsetto register,

[1] "*Soli margines videbantur agere*," *op. cit.* p. 58.

but in the latter the parts are altogether less tense, the vibration is more at the end of the glottis, and the upper orifice of the larynx is more open, so that the inside is better seen. Garcia conceived the fundamental difference between the chest and falsetto registers to lie in the (hypothetical) fact that in the former the arytenoid cartilages touch each other by the whole depth of the vocal process (anterior spur, see p. 178), whilst in the latter there is merely a contact of the edges. The resistance to the upward rush of the air would therefore be much greater in chest than in falsetto production. Garcia states that in the head voice the glottis becomes gradually shorter and narrower. It must be remembered that by his own avowal the discoverer of the laryngoscope never succeeded in seeing the anterior third of the glottis at all.[1] Battaille,[2] who although a singing master, had had a complete medical education, and had even been a professional teacher of anatomy, maintained that whereas in the production of chest notes the vocal ligaments vibrate in their entirety, and are extremely tense, especially in the antero-posterior direction, in the falsetto, on the other hand, the cords vibrate only at their free borders, and are altogether less tense. The difference between Battaille's view and that of Müller consists in this, that the former divides the vocal ligament into three parts, viz., subglottic, inner free border, and ventricular. In the chest register the subglottic part

[1] *Loc. cit.* p. 20.

[2] *Op. cit.*

vibrates with the rest, in the falsetto the other two alone come into play. Battaille gives an elaborate anatomical description of the subglottic part of the cord to which he attaches so much importance, but he has failed to inform us how he was able to see *below* the cords at a time when according to his own account they are in close apposition.

Mandl held that in the lower register the whole glottis is at first open and gradually closes posteriorly leaving a fairly wide elliptical opening between the cords, whereas in the higher register the edges of the glottis come so close together that there is only a linear interval between them. Mandl does not seem to have noticed the elliptical shape of the glottis which is characteristic of the head notes. Madame Seiler's observations are little more than a repetition of Garcia's as far as the chest and falsetto registers are concerned, but she was able to make a more minute study of the head notes. She says that in producing them the vibrating element is still further diminished owing to the posterior half of the vocal cords coming so tightly together as mutually to check each other's motion. Thus there remains an oval orifice corresponding to the front half of the glottis of which only the edges vibrate; this opening contracts and becomes more and more circular at every rise of tone.[1] Vacher[2] also made the difference of registers depend mainly on a variation in the length of the vibrating element.

[1] *Op. cit.* p. 59. [2] *Op. cit.*

Thus whilst the chest notes are produced by vibration of the whole length of the cord, from the arytenoid to its point of attachment to the thyroid cartilage, in the falsetto the cords come together in the greater part of their length but *vibrate* only in their anterior two thirds. The space between the inner surfaces of the arytenoid cartilages is according to him completely closed in *both* registers.

Behnke's view is in its main features identical with that of Madame Seiler ; he differs from her, however in one or two details, especially as regards the movements of the arytenoid cartilages. He demurs to the notion that these bodies which are merely pieces of gristle can *vibrate*, and he thinks that the difference between the chest and falsetto registers consists in a lessening of the tension of the vocal cords as the latter is exchanged for the former. As the pitch rises again, there is renewed tension, and then another factor comes in ; viz., gradual shortening of the vocal chink owing to the cords being pressed firmly together at the "ends."[1] From the figure of the "upper thin" register which accompanies this description I gather that Mr. Behnke means that the anterior as well as the hinder ends of the cords are approximated so as to check each other, the vibrating glottis being reduced to a small elliptical orifice, situated at about one quarter of the whole length of the cord from the front extremity.

[1] *The Mechanism of the Voice*, London, 1880, p. 88.

Dr. Illingworth's[1] theory (just referred to) as to the production of falsetto tones has at least the merit of novelty. In this gentleman's opinion it is the false vocal cords or ventricular bands (see p. 182) that are chiefly concerned in the process which is described as a kind of laryngeal *whistling*, the glottis playing the part of the whistler's mouth and the ventricular bands that of his lips. In the chest register Dr. Illingworth compares the action of the vocal organs to that of blowing a trumpet, the cords representing the lips of the player whilst the upper part of the larynx with the pharynx and mouth form the tube of the instrument.

Mr. Lunn[2] considers that in "true production" the ventricular bands, or false vocal cords, by separating only to a slight extent, exercise a restraining influence on the escape of vocalized air; whilst as regards the falsetto he has accepted[3] the views of Dr. Illingworth. Although it is highly probable that in the closure of the larynx, which takes place in the act of swallowing, the ventricular bands are closely approximated, I have never seen any such approximation, or, to use Mr. Lunn's words, slight separation, during singing or in ordinary phonation. Indeed, I may add that in the few cases in which I have seen the ventricular bands become approximated, laryngeal sound has always immediately ceased.

[1] *The Mechanism of the Voice*, Clayton le Moors, 1882.

[2] *Philosophy of Voice*, 5th edition, 1886, p. 20.

[3] *Op. cit.*

Dr. Wesley Mills's observations have a special importance on account of their comparatively extensive scale and the careful way in which they were conducted. Adopting Grützner's classification of "trained singers," "natural singers," and "non-singers," Dr. Mills examined fifty persons, and gives the result as far as could be ascertained in every case; it must be observed, however, that in a very large proportion of these subjects the action of the vocal cords could not be seen throughout the entire scale. Again, though I have no doubt that there are excellent singers in Montreal, it is not one of the places in which celebrated artists most do congregate. Indeed, amongst Dr. Mills's cases there were only ten trained singers, whilst there were twenty-one natural singers and nineteen non-singers. The result of the investigation was, therefore, somewhat incomplete as regards the working of the vocal reed in the singing voice.

Of the fifty cases thirty-seven were males and thirteen females. The whole glottis was open in all voices in the lowest tones of the chest register. This condition persisted up to  or thereabouts. Beyond this point the inter-cartilaginous part of the glottis closed, and the head-mechanism began, except in rare cases in which the chest adjustment was the only one used throughout the entire compass of the voice, owing either to natural endowment or a special method of teaching.

It is to be regretted I think that Dr. Mills has not more clearly defined the precise sense in which he uses the word "open" as applied to the glottis in singing, the term being liable to misconception, and to a person unacquainted with the subject even misleading. As already said the primary condition for the production of voice is approximation of the cords, and even in the deepest chest notes the aperture is so far closed that it is impossible to see *below* the glottis. We are, therefore, I presume, to understand the word "open" as equivalent to "not tightly closed," *i.e.* the cords are not actually touching, or at any rate are not in such close contact as to interfere with each other's mobility.

In connection with the question of the apposition of the vocal cords at their anterior extremities, Dr. Mills observed this action in many cases among the men whom he examined during the production of high falsetto notes: of thirteen women only three could make genuine head notes, and in two of these Dr. Mills was able to see the glottis distinctly, and he describes it as "more or less closed" at the anterior part, in fact offering just the same appearance as the male larynx in the high falsetto register. With regard to the theory that in falsetto only the thin edge vibrates, he pertinently asks, how much is implied in the term "edge"? Dr. Mills found that in the falsetto range the inter-cartilaginous glottis was always completely shut, and that the ligamentous glottis was also partly closed, the vocal cords being firmly pressed together behind, but in a variable degree in different persons. They were generally approximated in front as well this was invariably the case in the highest notes of the registers. Dr. Mills also concluded that the force of the blast, and the manner of blowing, are essential elements in falsetto production. He is strongly of opinion that *the high falsetto of men and the head voice of women are as regards mode of production practically identical.*

Martels[1] claims to have proved experimentally that in chest-singing it is only the mucous covering of the vocal cords that vibrates, not the substance of the ligaments themselves. The mucous membrane in that situation is, according to him, very loosely adherent to the parts which it covers, and if sound is produced in an exsected larynx by blowing through the windpipe, the membrane can be distinctly seen to detach itself from the underlying cord, and to take up a position in the glottis, where it vibrates. If the part which is thus seen to vibrate be pricked with a needle, the muscular tissue is never reached. Martels argues that the thyro-arytenoid muscle (see p. 183) in contracting bends the cords outwards a little, thus leaving an elliptical interval between their edges in the middle; the mucous membrane is thus slackened and set free to vibrate under the influence of the blast of air rushing through the glottis from below. The thyro-arytenoid in fact "prepares the way," but it is

[1] *Loc. cit.*

the crico-thyroid muscle (see p. 182) which actually produces song by giving the vocal membrane the length, breadth, and degree of tension required for each note. The difference between the chest and falsetto registers, according to Martels, is that, whilst the former is produced by *reeds*, the latter are in reality *flute* sounds. In falsetto it is not the membrane but the air itself which is the sounding body. He agrees with most of the other observers to whom I have alluded in affirming that in falsetto production the posterior part of the glottic chink is closed, and he says that at the same time the upper vocal cords (ventricular bands, see p. 182) contract and approach towards the middle line. The air-current after passing through the lower orifice (true glottis) strikes against the bevelled edges of the upper (formed, as just said, by the approximated edges of the ventricular bands). The higher the tone the smaller is the glottic orifice, and the closer together are the ventricular bands. Martels concludes therefore that the *upper glottis*, as he calls it, is the principal factor in falsetto, which in his view is synonymous with head production. Accordingly a singer whose ventricular bands are destroyed or immobilised by disease must be incapable of producing head notes.

MM. Gouguenheim and Lermoyez[1] sum up their view of the two different modes of production in the following formula, which, however, they are careful

[1] *Op. cit.* p. 149.

to point out must not be taken as a full and exact statement of the case:

Chest-voice = Larynx contracted + Pharynx relaxed.
Head-voice = Larynx relaxed + Pharynx contracted.

The main physiological features in head (falsetto) production, according to these writers, are first, relaxation of the glottis; secondly, shortening of its vibrating part. The relaxation of the cords by itself would of course according to the laws of physics *lower* the pitch. This difficulty is accordingly met by *shortening* the cords, which renders them capable of producing tones of a high pitch with less tension than would be necessary in cords of greater length. MM. Gouguenheim and Lermoyez lay much stress on the fact that there is a difference of timbre as well as of mere pitch between the two registers, and suggest that the peculiar quality of the falsetto, which is of a slender, flute-like character of sound with little reinforcement from harmonics, is due to: first, closure of the nasal passages by strong contraction of the soft palate; secondly, a special adjustment of the cavity of the mouth, the cheeks being more tense, and vibrating more freely than in the chest register. More recently M. Lermoyez in an independent work[1] expresses an altogether different opinion. He maintains that pitch is altered solely by *variation of tension* in the vocal cords, and agrees with Martels in explaining

[1] *Étude Expérimentale sur la Phonation*, Thèse de Paris, 1886, p. 199 *et seq.*

the difference between the chest and the head registers as owing to the fact that the *whole cord* vibrates in the former, and only the mucous membrane in the latter. Lermoyez now rejects the idea that the *length* of the reed has anything to do with the production of the difference.

From this brief review of the various scientific explanations that have been offered as to the production of the registers of the human voice, it will be seen that, setting aside all the confusion of terminology, and in spite of all the apparent discrepancies as to fact and the real divergences of opinion in the interpretation of them, there is much more agreement as to what is actually *seen* than at first sight seems to be the case. Leaving out of consideration mere eccentricities like Dr. Illingworth's trumpet-and-whistle theory, or subtleties like Dr. Martels's notion of a vibrating fringe, we find a pretty general consensus of testimony as to the essential *phenomena*, such as, first, the comparatively greater antero-posterior *tension* of the vocal cords in the chest register; secondly, the *smallness* of the glottic aperture in the head as contrasted with the chest register; thirdly, the smaller amount of substance thrown into vibration by the air-current in head tones. Another matter as to which there is perfect unanimity is that the air-blast is much less strong in head than in chest production. Every singer knows by his own experience that it is difficult to render a high chest note *piano*, and that the higher the pitch the less easy it becomes. It is, on the other hand almost impossible to sing a true falsetto note *forte.*

The chief points as to which there is disagreement are, first, the mutual relations of the arytenoid cartilages in the two registers; secondly, the contact or separation of the vocal cords at their anterior ends in head production; thirdly, the amount of vibrating substance in each respectively; fourthly, the action, or rather the changes of relative position in the parts above the glottis, especially the ventricular bands With regard to the first of these points every one admits that the vocal processes of the arytenoid cartilages come together at a certain part in the ascending scale in a large number of cases. Battaille, Vacher, Meyer, and MM. Gouguenheim and Lermoyez positively affirm that obliteration of that space by mutual apposition of the cartilages is a *sine quâ non* in phonation of any kind. Mandl, on the other hand, as we have seen, described the *whole glottis* as being slightly open during the emission of the lowest notes in the chest register. According to him the vocal processes do not touch each other till some progress has been made upwards, when the glottis has the appearance of being divided into an anterior and a posterior part. Mandl says that the posterior chink closes whilst the anterior diminishes in size, an account which as far as it goes coincides with that given by all other observers. Behnke remarks that according to his experience in the "lower thick" (lower chest) register, "there is as a rule a small triangular space between them (the arytenoid cartilages) which gets gradually smaller as the tones ascend until it is quite closed in the 'upper thick.' . . . . . Of this I can find no trace in the thin (falsetto) register."[1]

MM. Gouguenheim and Lermoyez ridicule Mandl's view that the cartilaginous glottis is open in the lower register, but both Wesley Mills and I (see Appendix III.) have found that this part of the glottis remains open until a certain point in the scale has been reached, and I have sometimes seen it open through the entire scale. Gouguenheim and Lermoyez are, however, so positive in affirming that without closure of that space no vocal sound is possible, that they say if their view on this point is false their whole teaching on the subject of the voice falls to pieces of itself. Lermoyez, however, in his more recent separate work already referred to has somewhat modified his view on this point.[2]

1 *Mechanism of the Human Voice*, London, 1880, p. 87.
2 *Étude Expérimentale sur la Phonation*, Paris, 1886, p. 200.

APPENDIX III.

THE POSITION OF THE VOCAL CORDS IN SINGING.

It has been objected to observations made with the laryngoscope, especially when the tongue is held out, that the action of the vocal cords is not precisely the same as when the voice is produced under more natural conditions, and Mr. Lunn[1] even doubts whether the vocal sounds of one of the most indefatigable autoscopic investigators possess any musical quality. The fact that the list given below contains observations made on the most celebrated professional and amateur singers of the day will show that a high standard of organ and a generally good mode of voice production has been taken.

The following are the names of some of the vocalists, *viz.*: Mesdames Nilsson, Albani, Valleria, Patey, Misses Anna Williams, Griswold, Ozelio, Carlotta Elliot, Florence St. John, Brandram, Jessie Bond and Fanny Leslie, (the late) Mr. Maas, Signor Foli, Messrs. Robertson, Ernest Birch, Charles Wade, Hayden Coffin, Corney Grain, Deane Brand, Bernard Lane, Hollins. and George Power. The amateurs include many of the best known singers in London. The observations made on many other well-known singers could not be made use of because it was not possible to see

[1] Lunn, *Artistic Voice in Speech and Song*, p. 15.

the working of the vocal cords through the entire scale. I do not consider myself competent to judge whether a given note possesses a high æsthetic quality, but in examining the celebrated singers who have kindly permitted me to study the action of their vocal cords, I have left it to them to determine when the note was good. Hence in my series of cases the objections urged by Mr. Lunn do not apply. The difficulties of making a laryngoscopic examination of the singing voice have already been pointed out (p. 18), but it may be added here that sometimes the mechanism seems to vary in the same individual on different occasions, and in a few persons the view is clear at one time and shut out at another.

In order to be able to tabulate fifty cases, between three and four hundred throats had to be examined, as in a large number of instances the act of singing could not be watched throughout the entire process. The cases now published were originally consecutive, but a few on the original list have been removed in order that the observations on more celebrated singers might be substituted The series of cases, however, must not be considered in any way *selected*, except in as far as the subjects have been chosen on account of their fine voices.

Before perusing the Tables, the reader is recommended to look once more at pp. 37—43.

Tab e show ng he shape of the glottis and condition of the voca cords dur ng s ng ng. In every case he compass has been es ed with he p ano, and he no e at wh ch cer a n descr bed changes have been observed has been subjec ed to he same est.

MALES.

No.	Voice.	Compass.	Sta e of Cartilaginous Glottis.	State of Ligamentous Glottis.	Remarks.
I.	Tenor. Trained.		Open o  closed above.	Gradual and complete c osure.	
II.	Tenor. Trained.		Open o  closed above.	Gradual and complete c osure.	

No.	Voice.	Compass.	State of Cartilaginous Glottis.	State of Ligamentous Glottis.	Remarks.
III.	Tenor. Trained.		 Open to  to closed 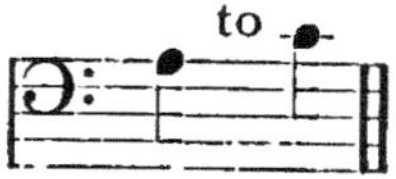 to stop-closed	Gradual closure; at  elliptical open anteriorly.	From 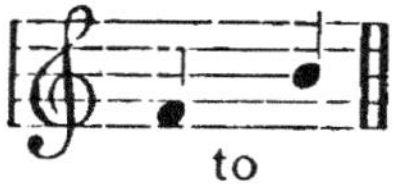 to distinctly falsetto in quality, and known to be so by singer.
IV.	Tenor. Trained.		Open up to  above that stop-closed.		
V.	Tenor. Trained.		Always closed.	Gradual closure.	

No.	Voice.	Compass.	Sta e of Cart.lagin.us Glottis.	State of Ligamentous Glottis.	Remarks.
VI.	Tenor. Trained.		Open o  closed above this.	Gradual, but complete closure.	
VII.	Tenor. Trained.		Open o  c osed a  stop-closed at 	Isosceles triangle to  above this elliptical opening occupying entire ligamentous glottis.	

No.	Voice.	Compass.	State of Cartilaginous Glottis.	State of Ligamentous Glottis.	Remarks.
VIII.	Tenor. Trained.		Always closed, but stop-closed from  to	Gradual and complete closure.	This singer has a greater compass than any whom I have examined.
IX.	Tenor. Trained.		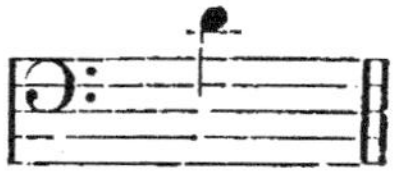 Open to closed above this.	Gradual complete closure.	
X.	Tenor. Trained.		 Open to closed above this.	Gradual complete closure.	
XI.	Tenor. Trained.		 Open to closed above.	Gradual, but complete closure.	

No.	Voice.	Compass.	State of Cartilaginous Glottis.	State of Ligamentous Glottis.	Remarks.
XII.	Barytone. Trained.		Closed throughou scale ; at  stop-closed ; above this "covered."[1]	At  closed anteriorly $\frac{1}{8}$th of an inch leaving elliptical opening.	
XIII.	Barytone. Natural.		Open o  c osed a  stop-c osed at 	Gradual closure ; elliptical opening at 	

1 Covered" means ha the capitula Santorini and he arytenoid cartilages in their upper part complete y cover he view of he back part of the glottis.

No.	Voice.	Compass.	State of Cartilaginous Glottis.	State of Ligamentous Glottis.	Remarks.
XIV.	Barytone. Natural.		Closed to  stop-closed in upper three notes.	Gradual closure; closed anteriorly in upper three notes  for about ⅛th of an inch.	No evidence of falsetto quality in upper three notes.
XV.	Barytone. Trained.		Open to  closed to  stop-closed above this; covered at 	Closed anteriorly in the whole of the upper octave.	Does not consider that the upper part of the voice is falsetto.

No.	Voice.	Compass.	Sta e of Cartilaginous Glottis.	S ate of Ligamentous Glottis.	Remarks.
XVI.	Barytone. Trained.		Open to  c osed to  above .his stop-closed.	In upper five notes el iptical opening in front. No c osure of voca cords an e- riorly.	
XVII.	Barytone.		Open o  closed above this.	Gradual bu com- plete c osure.	Notices himself a change of mechanism t 
XVIII.	Barytone. Trained.		Open o  closed above.	At  either gradual closure takes place, or an elliptical opening ac- cording to will.	In this case, the upper notes can be produced with either the long or short reed.

No.	Voice.	Compass.	State of Cartilaginous Glottis.	State of Ligamentous Glottis.	Remarks.
XIX.	Barytone. Trained.	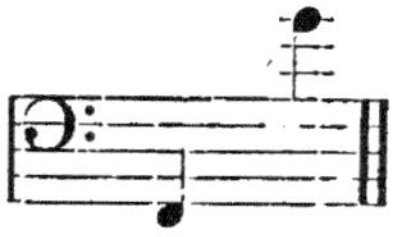	Open to 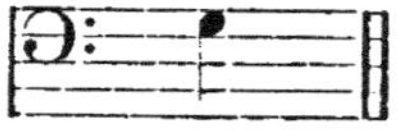	Gradual but complete closure.	
XX.	Barytone. Natural.	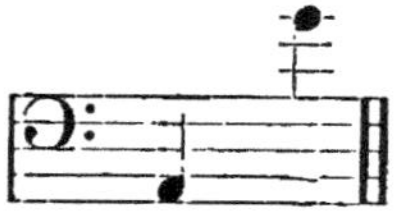	Open to 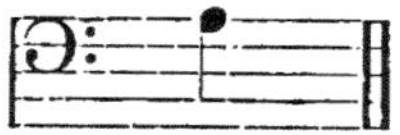	Gradual closure; from to 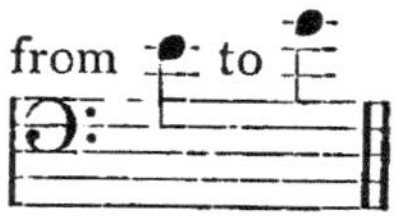 being completely closed.	
XXI.	Bass. Trained.	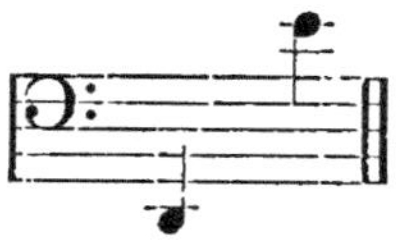 up to 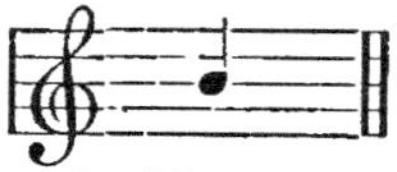 in falsetto.	Open to 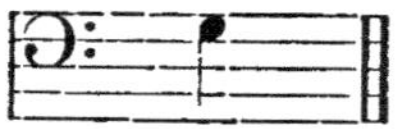 closed above; from 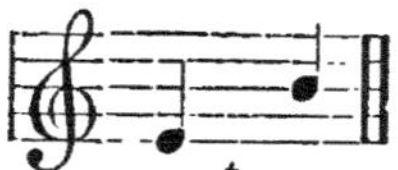 to stop-closed.	Closed in the upper five notes, elliptical opening commencing at anterior commissure.	

No.	Voice.	Compass.	State of Cartilaginous Glottis.	State of Ligamentous Glottis.	Remarks.
XXII.	Bass. Trained.		Open to  closed to  stop-closed to 	Never closed up to  above this, closure from before backwards.	Hooks the upper octave entirely falsetto. This singer is the most "popular entertainer" of the day; his powers of vocal mimicry being probably unsurpassed.
XXIII.	Bass. Trained.		Never closed.	Never quite closed.	
XXIV.	Bass. Trained.		Open to 	Never completely closed.	
XXV.	Bass. Trained.		Closed when note is sustained; but remains open in staccato note throughout.	Never completely closed.	Arytenoid seen to vibrate very distinctly in lower notes.

FEMALES.

No.	Voice.	Compass.	State of Cartilaginous Glottis.	State of Ligamentous Glottis.	Remarks.
I.	Soprano. Trained.	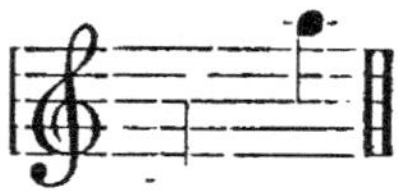	Open at  Closed at  stop-closed at 	Partial closure, but elliptical opening at 	Notices that the head voice commences at  Notices change of sensation in throat at 
II.	Soprano. Trained.		Closed throughout scale.	Complete closure.	

No.	Voice.	Compass.	State of Cartilaginous Glottis.	State of Ligamentous Glottis.	Remarks.
III.	Soprano. Trained.		Open throughout	Partial approximation, but never complete closure.	Thinks that the notes above  are head notes, but this view is not supported by laryngoscopic observation.
IV.	Soprano. Trained.		Open to  closed above.	Gradual complete closure.	
V.	Soprano. Trained.		Closed throughout	Gradual and complete closure, so that in upper four notes the line of demarcation is scarcely distinguishable between the cords.	

No.	Voice.	Compass.	State of Cartilaginous Glottis.	State of Ligamentous Glottis.	Remarks.
VI.	Soprano. Trained.		Open to; closed to; stop-closed above this.	Glottal closure, but never complete; slight elliptical opening remaining in upper three notes.	
VII.	Soprano. Trained.		Open to	Never quite closed.	
VIII.	Soprano. Trained.		Open to; closed above this.	Never quite closed.	Considers [illegible] from [illegible] are [illegible], and they have this quality, but there is no elliptical opening

No.	Voice.	[illegible]	State of Cartilaginous Glottis.	State of Ligamentous Glottis.	Remarks.
IX.	Soprano. [illegible]	[staff notation]	Open to [staff notation] closed above this.	Gradual approximation, but never completely closed.	Considers [illegible] form [staff notation] are h[illegible] not [illegible]
X.	Soprano. [illegible]	[staff notation]	Open [illegible] [staff notation] closed above.	[illegible] approximation, but never complete closure.	
XI.	Soprano. [illegible]	[staff notation]	Open [illegible] [staff notation] [illegible]	[illegible] [illegible] m[illegible], but never complete c[illegible]	

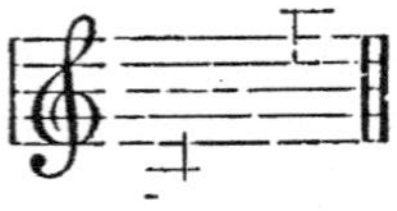

No.	Voice.	Compass.	State of Cartilaginous Glottis.	State of Ligamentous Glottis.	Remarks.
XII.	Mezzo-Soprano. Natural.		Open to closed above this.	Gradual and complete closure.	
XIII.	Mezzo-Soprano. Natural.		Closed throughout scale; stop-closed at closed above this point.	Gradual closure, with closure anteriorly to ⅛th of an inch in upper notes.	
XIV.	Mezzo-Soprano. Trained.		Open to closed above this.	Gradual and complete closure.	Thinks the upper three notes are head notes.

Q

No.	Voice.	Compass.	State of Cartilaginous Glottis.	State of Ligamentous Glottis.	Remarks.
XV.	Mezzo-Soprano. Trained.		Open to closed above.	Gradual and complete.	Notices a change between and again between no corresponding change seen with the mirror.
XVI.	Mezzo-Soprano. Trained.		Open to closed above.	Never closed.	Feels that a change of register always takes place at about but no corresponding change seen with laryngoscope.

No.	Voice.	Compass.	State of Cartilaginous Glottis.	State of Ligamentous Glottis.	Remarks.
XVII.	Mezzo-Soprano. Trained.		Open to closed to stop-closed to above this closed.	Gradual closure to above this a vanishing elliptical opening.	
XVIII.	Mezzo-Soprano. Natural.		Open to closed above this to stop-closure at	From sometimes gradual complete closure takes place; at other times a small opening is left, the vocal cords being approximated to $\frac{1}{16}$th of an inch anteriorly, and posteriorly for rather less than $\frac{3}{8}$th of an inch.	

No.	Voice.	Compass.	Sta e o Cartilaginous Glottis.	Sta e of Ligamentous Glottis.	Remarks.
XIX.	Mezzo-Soprano. Trained.		pOre to  c sed o  stop-c sed to  covered above this.	Gradual ha, but anterior elliptical opening in upper oc a.	
XX.	Contralto. Trained.		pOre o  sed abe this.	Never closed in any part of the scale.	Thinks ha a change of register takes lpce when 

No.	Voice.	Compass.	State of Cartilaginous Glottis.	State of Ligamentous Glottis.	Remarks.
XXI.	Contralto. Trained.		Never closed	Never completely closed.	Considers that a change takes place at
XXII.	Contralto. Trained.		Open to closed above this.	Gradual and regular closure, opening of glottis disappearing as a vanishing isosceles triangle.	Thinks that is a different register and that another change takes place at but no corresponding changes are observed with the laryngoscope.

No.	Voice.	Compass.	State of Cartilaginous Glottis.	State of Ligamentous Glottis.	Remarks.
XXIII.	Contralto. Natural.		Never closed.	[Gradual] closure.	
XXIV.	Contralto. Trained.		Never closed. (A good instrument.)	Never closed.	
XXV.	Contralto. Trained.		Open to  / closed to  / stop-closed to  / above this covered.	Until [illegible] closure with [a diminishing] elliptical opening.	

INDEXES.

INDEX OF SUBJECTS.

A.

B.

C.

INDEX OF NAMES.

Richard Clay and Sons,
LONDON AND BUNGAY.

WORKS BY THE SAME AUTHOR,

PUBLISHED BY

J. & A. CHURCHILL, NEW BURLINGTON STREET.

DISEASES OF THE THROAT AND NOSE.

Vol I.—PHARYNX, LARYNX, and TRACHEA.

With 112 Illustrations, post 8vo, 12*s.* 6*d.*

OPINIONS OF THE PRESS.

"The outcome of Dr. Mackenzie's unrivalled experience of the affections of which he treats."—*Medical Times and Gazette.*

"There can be but one verdict of the profession on this manual—it stands without any competitor in British medical literature as a standard work on the organs it professes to treat of."—*Dublin Journal of Medical Science.*

"For clear style and keen close analysis of the whole bearings of each department of the subject, this book must be allowed to stand in the highest rank of English contributions to medical science; while the extensive experience of the author, handled in his well-known candid and independent way, gives the greatest force to the conclusions arrived at."—*Glasgow Medical Journal.*

"Dr. Mackenzie's work is classic."—*New York Medical Record.*

"Le nom seul de son auteur est un sûr garant de sa valeur scientifique."—*Union Médicale.*

"Die Summe seiner reichen Erfahrungen und Studien."—*Zeitschrift für Klin. Med.*

Vol. II.—ŒSOPHAGUS, NOSE, and NASO-PHARYNX.

With 93 Illustrations, post 8vo, 12*s.* 6*d.*

OPINIONS OF THE PRESS.

"Some of the special features of this work are its wealth of accurate reference to related literature; its carefully-planned histories of the various diseases; the conciseness and clearness of its language, and the thoroughness of its pathology, so far as that is possible."—*Lancet.*

"It is needless to say that, coming from the pen of one with so large an experience of diseases of the throat as Dr. Mackenzie, the book is of great value; but this value is considerably enhanced by the amount of care and labour that it has evidently received."—*British Medical Journal.*

R

"We cannot but admire the splendid industry and perseverance which have been combined to place before the profession so complete and scholarly a summary of such a wide and varied field of research." —*Medical Times.*

"In concluding, we would wish to say that this book is one that should be on the table of every medical man, whether he be surgeon, physician, or specialist. He can read the book for pleasure or for information, or use it as a dictionary when in a difficulty."—*Medical Press and Circular.*

"Altogether, we have no hesitation in repeating our high estimate of the value of the work, the production of which confirms what has long been the opinion of the profession, that its author is the most erudite and skilful laryngologist of the present time."—*Edinburgh Medical Journal.*

"We can safely say of this, the completed work, that it is a marvel of skill, a monument of patient labour, and an evidence of that thought, care, and able observation which has made the name of Mackenzie famous for now nearly a quarter of a century."—*Birmingham Medical Review.*

"The book is in no sense a compilation. Whilst giving proof of learning at once extensive and discriminating, it is, above all, a record of the author's personal experience. As this brief notice itself shows, his task has been undertaken only after mature thought and prolonged practical study. The preface tells us how many years were required to produce a work conceived on so vast a scale, so replete with facts, so detailed and precise in its teaching."—*Union Médicale.*

"Taking this work on the Throat and Nose altogether, there can be but one opinion in regard to it. It is a credit to medical literature, and will always occupy a place among the standard works. As a text-book it is exhaustive and reliable; in short, the best in our judgment which at present exists in any language."—*Boston Medical and Surgical Journal.*

ESSAYS ON THROAT DISEASES.

ESSAY No. I. 8vo, 3s. 6d.

HOARSENESS, LOSS OF VOICE.

OPINIONS OF THE PRESS.

(Second Edition.)

"No one has done more than Dr. Mackenzie to elucidate the pathology and treatment of diseases of the throat and air-passages so common in our climate. . . . . The book is one which deserves the attention of the profession."—*British Medical Journal.*

"Dr. Mackenzie has worked in a new field in a scientific spirit, and the profession is under a great obligation to him for the progress he has already made in this unexplored region of clinical research."—*Medical Times and Gazette.*

"The cases recorded are instructive, and are thoroughly illustrative of the value of electricity in many forms of aphonia."—*Practitioner.*

ESSAY No. II. Profusely Illustrated with Wood Engravings and Chromo-Lithographs, 8vo, 12s. 6d.

GROWTHS in the LARYNX; with Reports and an Analysis of One Hundred Consecutive Cases treated by the Author.

OPINIONS OF THE PRESS.

"Dr. Mackenzie shows possession of what has been well called the complete professional mind."—*Lancet.*

"The most complete and original essay on new formations in the larynx."—*Medical Times and Gazette.*

"A model of honest and complete work, and honourable to British medicine, as it is useful to practitioners of every country."—*British Medical Journal.*

"This work will certainly at once take its place as the author's chief one, and on it alone he may be content to let his reputation rest. . . . . . The book is as complete as it is possible to make it." *Medical Press.*

"The entire profession is under a deep obligation to Dr. Mackenzie for his really interesting, instructive, and opportune essay."—*Edinburgh Medical Journal.*

"The essay can hardly fail to increase Dr. Mackenzie's already honourable position as an accomplished laryngologist and instructor. We trust that the work will find readers not only among physicians especially interested in the subject of which it treats, but among general practitioners as well. They will find it particularly free from the technicalities which often make works on special subjects dull reading."—*American Journal of Medical Science.*

ESSAY No. III. Post 8vo, 5s.

DIPHTHERIA; Its Nature and Treatment. Varieties and Local Expressions.

OPINIONS OF THE PRESS.

"One of the best and most complete essays ever written."—*London Medical Record.*

"The chapter on treatment is especially valuable."—*Medical Times and Gazette.*

"This little book is of a type which it might be wished were more commonly to be met with among medical works of the day."—*Athenæum.*

"The outcome of his ripe experience."—*New York Medical Journal.*

"Exhibits the accuracy, care, fullness of research, and facility of condensation displayed by its author in previous essays."—*American Journal of Medical Science.*

"En résumé, le Docteur Morell Mackenzie a réuni en une intéressante monographie les données de la science contemporaine sur la diphthérie, en les éclairant et les enrichissant par l'intelligente addition des résultats de son expérience personelle si spéciale et si étendue."—*Union Médicale.*

"Un vero quadro parlante."—*Gazzetta degli Ospedali.*

"Merita di essere raccomandato specialmente per il carattere scientifico che lo informa intimamente connesso con quel fino senso pratico, di cui sono maestri gli Inglesi, e par lá vasta erudizione che contiene, facendo tesoro di quanto in questi ultimi tempi è stato scritto di meglio, non solo in Inghilterra, ma in tutto il mondo civile."—*L'Imparziale.*

HAY FEVER; ITS ETIOLOGY AND TREATMENT.

WITH AN APPENDIX ON ROSE COLD.

Third Edition. 8vo, Price 2s. 6d.

"This is a condensed, but very complete, account of a most interesting pathological condition, the subject being treated with that conscientious thoroughness which distinguishes all Dr. Mackenzie's literary work." *Medical Times and Gazette.*

"We have, put together in a concise and most interesting form, all that is known of the disease up to the present, and we strongly recommend it to those who take an interest in this affection, whether personally or professionally."—*Medical Press and Circular.*

"Those who are interested in the subject of hay fever will find in this little pamphlet a brief but comprehensive account of all that is known about it. To the general practitioner, who must often be at a loss in dealing with cases of this kind, the present communication (coming as it does from one of the highest authorities) is likely to prove highly serviceable, and we have pleasure in recommending it."—*Glasgow Medical Journal.*

"The learned author, moreover, gives evidence of no mean literary skill, and writes with a 'lucidity' that should delight the heart of Mr. Matthew Arnold."—*Sunday Times.*

"Nous recommandons la lecture de la brochure de M. Morell Mackenzie, qui est agréable et instructive."—*Union Médicale.*

"In dieser Broschüre giebt uns Dr. Morell Mackenzie, der ausgezeichnete englische Specialist fur die Krankheiten der Athmungsorgane, einen vollständigen und klaren Bericht über Heufieber."—*Wiener Medizinische Zeitung.*

CPSIA information can be obtained
at www.ICGtesting.com
Printed in the USA
LVOW04s1526080316
478282LV00020B/896/P

9 781330 267578